YIKES!!

my butt's fallin|||
g

Humerous *"tails"* of aging
baby boomers

Aleta Pippin & Robyn Mulhearn

Inner Sources Publishing
La Jolla, California

Cover design and Illustrations: Autumn Lew, Graphic Minion Studios, San Diego

Inner Sources Publishing, California

Publisher's Cataloging-in-Publication Data
(Provided by Quality Books, Inc.)

Pippin, Aleta.
   Yikes!! my butt's falling : humorous "tails" of aging boomers / Aleta Pippin & Robyn Mulhearn. -- 2nd ed.
   p. cm.
   LCCN: 99-94066
   ISBN: 0-9660546-3-6

   1. Baby boom generation—Humor. 2. Aging--Humor.
I. Mulhearn, Robyn. II. Title.

PN6231.B22P57 2000   813'.54
                           QBI99-500278

Published in the United States.

Dedication

To our Mommies and Daddies for having sex at the right moment, qualifying us as baby boomers.

To God for your sense of humor. Sorry if we got some of it wrong. That's what happens when you talk to humans.

Table of Contents

Acknowledgement

Introduction
I'm 50. The number flattens
me like a steamroller!
Page 11

I. Baby Boomers
They should call us aging boomers.
Page 19

II. Down the Up StairMaster
My butt's as big as a house.
Page 35

III. To Eat Or Not To Eat...
Why does it have to be so
hard to look good?
Page 51

IV. Plastic Splurgery
Nipped, Sucked, Tucked,
and Plucked
Page 71

V. Hormonal Hell
*Is it my hormones
or am I just a bitch?*
Page 83

VI. Tick, Tock - Baby Begot
Beat the clock
Page 97

VII. To Wear a Toup Or Not...That Is the Question
Male Pattern Baldness - Is it contagious?
Page 105

VIII. Prozac - the New Wonder Drug
All psyched up and nowhere to go.
Page 119

IX. God...Help Me!!
Why am I here?
Page 131

X. You Mean It's Okay to Enjoy Life?
It's about time you figured it out!
Page 143

Acknowledgment

We want to acknowledge Carolyn Doherty, Jeanne Isgro, and Melissa Pippin for sacrificing themselves to read this book. Thanks to Rania Culbreth for her assistance with Corel Draw. Special thanks to Laura Weaver for her meaningful suggestions, and to Corky Weaver for reading the book three times (masochist) and, good-naturedly, putting up with our chatter and laughter while we were writing it.

Special thanks to Frank King, White Collar Comedy, for finding the jokes we missed. And to Autumn Lew, Graphic Minion Studios, for her illustrative work ...so in sync with our humor.

We would like to explain to all of our friends who will claim they're the interviewees, *we have never seen these people before*.

Introduction

I'm 50.
The number
flattens me
like a steamroller.

I'm fifty. *50.* The number flattens me like a steamroller. (Do they still use those? Or is that just another example of how old I am?) When I was a kid, fifty was Ancient. Fifty year-old women were matrons who wore corsets over their swelling bottoms, dork-o-pedic shoes on their feet, and had personally witnessed the building of the Pyramids. They certainly didn't wear jeans and sweatshirts, didn't start new careers, and definitely didn't read books on dating.

I *cannot* be fifty! Although the image in the mirror is showing some wear, sagging here, wrinkled there, and graying almost everywhere (under the shampoo-in hair color), I'm still pretty fit and trim, look 40-ish, and wear a size four. My blue eyes still know how to flash provocatively when the right man glances my way. (Assuming I've got my glasses on and I can *see* him do it.) So, how could I be fifty?

If I could, I'd like to get an appointment with God and talk about this. Yes. I know. A lot of you are going to tell me that appointments with God should be reserved for more important occurrences. Like when your dog just got hit by a car and is in surgery, the balloon payment on your mortgage comes due, and your daughter's sixteenth birthday party ("Mom," spoken beseechingly, "I'll only be sixteen once in my whole life!") all hit in the same month.

But in these many years leading up to this one, I've decided a few things. One of them is that God should be able to meet with you at any time, for any reason. After all, he is God, isn't he? He's capable of everything and anything. So turning fifty should be one of those things that you can discuss with him. I can imagine the discussion going a little like this:

                                                       ॐ   ॐ   ॐ   ॐ   ॐ   ॐ

Listen, God, I need to talk to you.

Yes.

(Gulp!!) You're here.

Yes.

I mean...really here.

Yes, my child. I heard your pitifully pleading call. By the way, I don't usually respond to that tone, since I'm more attuned to those of you wanting help to experience personal growth, not personal anguish.

This is about growth! I'm growing old...just look at me! Look at these crow's feet!

Those do look pretty grim. Hey, I know a plastic surgeon that gives discounts to Christians on Wednesdays. Mention my name.

Is he good?

Would I lead you astray? In a previous

life he performed a makeover on Methuse-
lah, who never looked a day over 250,
even at his death. Of course, now he only
allows one hour for each operation.
Doesn't want to be late for his tee-off time.

Thanks, but how about just performing one of those
miracles you're so famous for? I'm short of cash right now.

I sent a do-it-yourself book down so you
could create your own miracles. Tells you
all about how to do it. It's called *A Course
in Miracles.* Good book - if I do say so
myself. Although I don't remember a
chapter on plastic surgery.

Yes, I've read it. But I've been really busy, and that
stuff is complicated. Why, I could spend from here to eternity
just learning how to do it. Couldn't you just give me a quickie
to help me along? Maybe just one eye to start? You
know…that's not the only problem I have. There's the sciatica,
and the spur on my heel…

Hey, if I personally helped every one of
you, I'd have no time to create new worlds,
talk shop with the angels, counsel St. Pete
about his gate-keeping skills, etc. Why,
just last week he got into it with an IRS

How 'bout a little quickie around the eyes to help me along?

agent from Poughkeepsie (don't ask me how an IRS agent got as far as the gates), and...

That's okay. I guess I'll just have to handle this age thing on my own. You seem too busy. Sorry. I never imagined that God would be *too* preoccupied to help one of his children. I thought that's what you're around for.

I am. But I also expect you to help

---

yourselves. I've sent you all kinds of knowledge: Oprah's Book Club, The Jerry Springer Show, The National Enquirer, even the whole New Age movement. (Although Yanni wasn't my idea.) What more can a God do? You have to take some responsibility for yourselves.

It wasn't me who chose to go sky-diving to impress that guy you were dating. Or wore those shoes that pinched, just because they matched that blue suit. Or laid in the sun covered only with Crisco, frying like bacon. No, all of you knew that those decisions and the age thing were going to catch up to you. Just because you call yourselves *baby* boomers doesn't mean that you're immune to the whole cycle-of-life thing. Get real!

Uh, sorry about that. So I'm just stuck with this age thing, that's what you're saying, huh?

And Satan says humans don't catch on fast! Like I said, I know this plastic surgeon...

❧   ❧   ❧   ❧   ❧   ❧

A friend recently pointed out that, according to Internet stats, there are seventy-eight million baby boomers mixing it up in today's society. That's a lot of matrons, with a few middle-aged Lotharios thrown in, to complete the pudding. I think that most of them are just like me, wondering how this could have happened to our generation, the first group of humans to actively seek, as a whole, every fountain of youth promise to come down the pike, including Thighmaster, Gutbuster and that Asian cellulite removing soap. So I thought, "let's take a look at this phenomenon, and talk to some of the people caught up in it."

I took a pencil and a pad, and started talking to friends. As it turns out, I seem to know a lot of baby boomers. Perhaps we seek each other out in order to boost our sagging morales, not to mention other pertinent parts of our anatomy. Perhaps it's simply that there are so many of us. We certainly feel more comfortable with those who have similar problems. We also get a boost from recognizing that some have it much worse than we do. But when we find those who are better off, it's worse than a bad hair day, discovering that your husband left you, and that Paul Newman's gay, all rolled into one. (Note: Paul Newman's definitely not gay, not that there's anything wrong with that.)

Fortunately, I was to find that most of us are in the same boat. It's an aging, sagging, weather-beaten boat, but we're all in it just the same. Read on and you'll see what I mean.

I. Baby Boomers

...they should call us *aging* boomers
rather than *baby* boomers.

I decided to begin my research at the local coffee house. Many artsy-fartsy types hang out there, talking about their latest and greatest. It's my favorite hangout, a place where I can sit quietly or find someone to chat with, if that's my desire. Today, I definitely needed to ponder. This whole baby boomer aging dilemma had taken me completely off guard.

I was surprised to find out, during my Internet research, that every seven and a half seconds a boomer turns 50. (There goes one now!) Whew! *Imagine...78 million boomers jogging along the treadmill toward middle age, one turning 50 every seven and a half seconds!* (There goes another one!) Now *that's* a scary thought. Worse yet, I'm one of those who's seven and a half seconds have already come and gone.

I never thought *I'd* get to this stage of life *so soon*. Oh look, there's God again. Might as well start at the top with my interviews. This is getting to be a regular occurrence.

∼ ∼ ∼ ∼ ∼ ∼

You rang?

I didn't know you'd be here!

Of course I'm here. I'm everywhere.

Since you're here, tell me...what's the deal with this aging thing?

You think you've got it bad turning a mere fifty? I've turned fifty at least a gazillion times over. So what can I do for you?

You've always gotta one-up me, don't you?

Hey watch the attitude. Remember I
brought you into this world and I can take
you right back out.

Sorry. This age thing is really getting me down. Why, only yesterday we were protesting a war and staging love-ins, or doing both at the same time at that great demonstration of brotherly love - Woodstock. (Chuckling) Remember all those people over thirty we couldn't trust? They were convinced it would turn into a mass riot. They couldn't imagine *that* many people uniting without causing trouble.

So, God, what did *you* think of the hippies?

I thought they were real kool, man, the
greatest, the hippest, the most enlightened
(up to that point) people...

Okay, okay. I get your point. But, if you thought they were so kool, why did you have it rain on their parade - Woodstock?

Don't you read your Bible - "Into every
life a little rain must fall."

That's not in the Bible.

Oops! Well, I'm surprised. The writers put everything else they could think of in there!

Back to your question...I think you're all great. You know, it reminds me of the old days when Jesus delivered his "Sermon on the Mount." There were a multitude of people there. (Although Hendrix and Joplin didn't show.)

Of course, there weren't as many people as Woodstock, but then there weren't as many people. Those who did attend Jesus's sermon were well-behaved, giving love, and all that. Even sharing their food.

Wait a minute. I thought Jesus made the food appear out of thin air?!

There are miracles and there are "miracles." You want the sensational ones. But thousands of people quietly sharing is more of a miracle than Jesus waving his hands over some fishes, and loaves, and turning them into the world's first "all you can eat" buffet. Doesn't that make sense?

You know, I've always wondered about that whole miracle thing.

And miracles are still happening.

Yeah...I read about them all the time in The Star... *Bigfoot's Having My Baby!*

But see, you're still looking for sensation-alism. Jesus said, "...even greater things will you do." Look around. You've learned to utilize electricity, microwaves and lasers.

Not to mention the Flow-bee, Ginsu Knife and spray on hair.

You've learned to fly. Well...everybody but Value Jet. You have technology that con-nects you around the world in seconds. You can even destroy the planet instantly.

Thanks for the thoughts. All that's true but it's a little more than I wanted to know. We're getting off track here. What did you *really* think of the hippies?

That is so human. I'm sharing these won-derful thoughts with you and all you want to know about is my opinion of the hippies? I loved them. I loved their free and easy spirit. Reminded me of myself.

Ummmm…made in your image…

Bingo! That ol' Satan is wrong after all. You humans aren't really slow learners.

As I contemplated my conversation with the Lord of Hosts, I spotted my old friend, George, a tall muscular man in his early 50's. He looked as if he spent every waking moment at the health club. Why hadn't I thought of George before? He'd make a great contributor to my book on baby boomers and aging. Not having seen him for several months, I waved him over. "George, how ya doing?"

George, with a big grin on his face, ambled toward my table. "Great!"

Yeah, George was always doing great. Lucky guy. He had an extremely successful business, having developed a sophisticated self-management program. His avocation was writing poetry, which seemed incongruent with his physique. That sensitive side must work though, because he'd just hooked a beautiful blonde, Jasmine. He does seem to have one minor problem - marriage. Jasmine is his third wife. I'm not sure what that's about, except when his first and second wives neared 40, he started looking around. It seems his self-management program has not extended into his personal life.

"Hey, how'd you like to have a cup of coffee and catch me up on what's been happenin' with you?" I asked.

"Yeah. I've got an hour or so to kill."

The waitperson meandered over to take our order. (What's wrong with these kids today? They simply don't have the snap we had when we were their age. Listen to me "with these kids today"...I'm even talking old. I can remember my mom saying that when I was sixteen...which was - *Oh God! - 34 years ago*...) I ordered a cool mocha and George ordered a latte.

"So how've you been?" George asked.

"Really good. I'm working on a book about the "tails" of aging boomers. You can help me by being an interviewee," I said.

"Well...maybe." George looked doubtful. "What do I have to do?"

"Just share some of your feelings with me. For instance, how *do* you feel about aging? About being middle-aged?" George looked away, his eyes glazing over as he glanced out the window. I knew I'd hit a hot button with him. "Hey George, George - are you there?"

"I'm afraid I can't help you. I haven't hit middle age yet." (I'm thinking, "yes you have" unless you're planning to live to be 140.)

I knew better than to do the math for George and point out the fact that he had children from his first wife who were now married and having children of their own. I guess in George's mind becoming a Grandfather doesn't qualify you as middle-aged.

Maybe George had unwittingly helped with my project after all. I wondered how many other baby boomers are in denial about their age? I changed the subject. "So George, what've you been up to?"

George turned back to me, a big grin crossing his face. "Man, I had the best weekend. Jasmine and I took a walk down memory lane. We attended a Woodstock reunion!"

I doubt Jasmine was at Woodstock, unless it was in her mother's womb. I'm guessing that until she met George, she thought Woodstock was that little bird in Peanuts. "No kidding! I hadn't heard anything about it. How was it?"

"Fantastic! You know I was fortunate enough to attend the original and this was just like being there again."

"You mean you took your little pup tent and camped out under the stars, taking only the clothes you had on, and not bathing the entire weekend? And what about drugs? You're not still into drugs are you?" (Other than Viagra.)

"Well...it may have been a little different. You know Jasmine and I like to have our sex in a comfortable bed. (Yeah...well, I gathered Jasmine likes being comfortable, that's why she married a guy with money who is twice her age.)

Besides that, I haven't owned a pup tent since the early 70's. No, we went in our new R.V."

This didn't seem *exactly* like being there the first time to me, but I didn't want to burst George's bubble. "So George, tell me about your adventure." Though this wasn't about the aging thing, you never know what little tidbit of useful information you'll glean from a good story.

"As I said, Jasmine and I like our creature comforts. Besides, there're some really good shows on TV Friday evenings I don't want to miss. (Like what? Sabrina the Teenage Witch?) So it was essential that we take the R.V. It was either that or not go. An added benefit was having all the other goodies, you know, CD player, VCR, laptop. That way I could stay in touch with what's going on in the world. You never know when something important is going to happen."

This didn't sound *anything* like the old Woodstock to me. At that one, people didn't seem the least bit concerned if they missed the news. Fact is, they were the news. You'll also recall it rained most of the time. People were O.D.'ing on drugs, lying around in muddy fields, and to top it all off, the facilities were in short supply *and* overloaded.

I don't know why George thought this trip was so reminiscent of that first adventure. Maybe, at the original Woodstock, he was on LSD and hallucinated throughout the entire event that he was in an R.V. Maybe his body was at Woodstock but his mind wasn't. Oops! My mind's obviously not with George, he's still prattling on. I wondered if I missed anything important, or in his case self-important.

"Yeah, it was so cool. Just like before. People were so friendly, talking to each other and all. I told Jasmine this would be a bitchin' time. We bicycled and jogged. Some people brought their rollerblades and went over to a paved parking area. I led a group in Tai Chi."

I just had to ask. "Did you enjoy these activities in the buff? After all, at the original Woodstock there were many people letting, shall we say, 'the sun shine in'." I smirked.

"No way. Don't you know that sun is lethal?" (Gees...George is even older than I thought!)

"Well, I just had to ask. Like I said, lots of people were nude. Or have you forgotten?"

"Hey, I have a great memory. (Thanks, no doubt to ginko biloba. If that were true you'd remember you were pulling 50 not pushing it, and would have reframed from marrying a woman half your age who'd be surprised to find out that Paul McCartney was in a band *before* "Wings.") No, we didn't get naked. You know that's not really acceptable anymore. Besides, it would just mean having to put sunblock on more body parts, which might be fun. Actually, I don't want the sun to age me before my time. (Hey pal, your watch has stopped. You're past your time.) You know, when I finally do reach middle-age, I'd rather people believe I'm younger. In fact, Jasmine and I have a little routine we do every morning. I rub sunblock on her and she rubs it on me."

"Is that all you do to protect yourself?" I visualized their sunblock rubbing routine and the possibilities.

"No, whenever I'm outside for a long time, I wear my hat and shades. And to top it off, I recently discovered special sunblock clothing. So, at the Woodstock reunion, I was fairly protected by the time the music began. I'd filled my cooler with a six-pack of Evian Water, gotten out my favorite lounge chair, set it up in the shade of the awning, and relaxed. (That's really roughing it!) Of course, I protected my hearing with specially-made earplugs."

"Earplugs?! You've got to be kidding." I eyed George incredulously. "When did you start using those things?"

George turned deadly serious. "You know, you can't be too safe these days. That music gets cranked up pretty loudly. You should really consider earplugs. It'll protect your hearing as you go into *your* senior years." (Oh *I'm* middle aged and you're not? Oh *I'll* be a senior before you? Then let's do the math and see who'll really be leading that parade. We'll figure out who already received their first piece of mail from AARP.)

George continued, "I take mine everywhere. They really come in handy at theaters with those new surround sound systems blasting out at high volume. Gees, I hate that. I'd wear them when I'm driving if I thought I could get away with it. Even more than surround sound, I hate the boom, boom, boom of the base speakers those snot-nosed kids put in their cars."

I couldn't believe George said that about the earplugs *or* the over-sized speakers in the cars. Not George! In college, he was one of those guys who drove a VW van with a boom box, including an eight-track player, and bed in the back, just in case. His motto - 'be prepared, you never know when you might get lucky.' I blurted out, "George, you're really getting conservative. I thought you loved loud music!"

"I do. But I want to have my hearing when I get old."

Yeah...earplugs would go nicely with those blinders you're wearing. The ones that won't let you see the truth about your mortality. A 30 year old wife doesn't make you young, she just gives you a good-looking widow.

I was really loving this. George was going to turn out to be like so many of us baby boomers, seeing himself young, yet becoming rigid in his thinking. This couldn't have been better fodder for my book if I'd planned it.

"George, how about food at the reunion? Did they bring in all those greasy concession stands like before?"

"Nah. Natural food stores, like Wild Oats and Whole Foods. You should have seen their selection of organic fruits and vegetables. Fantastic. Though I have to admit to liking a big ol' juicy steak once in a while. I figured this would be the perfect time to try out a portable grill I'd just bought.

"Boy was I wrong! It was a nightmare. Here I am, minding my own business. I've set the new grill up in the shade of the R.V., just waiting for the charcoal to get hot. I'm feeling like the king of my domain. Just as I'm getting ready to slap two big ol' chunks of meat down on the grill, this really skinny little gal jogs by. I'm pleasant enough, gesturing with my tongs, nodding 'hello.'

"For some reason she comes to a screeching halt just beyond the grill. I'm thinking maybe she pulled something and I ask her if I can help. I'm taken completely off guard when she asks me what in the hell I'm doing. I'm wondering what her problem is but not wanting to create any trouble, in a nice tone I reply, 'I'm getting ready to barbecue.'

"She gets all red in the face and I wonder if she's choking and needs some water. Nope. That's not the problem. She goes off on me - 'don't I know the rain forests are in jeopardy because of all of us scum-bag meat-eaters? Don't I know they're clearing forests to pasture cows - those stinky, smelly creatures who pollute the air with their farts? What's wrong with me?'" George paused for affect.

Then he continued in earnest, "Well, by now I'm thinking she's half a bubble off and wished she'd just leave. No way. She tells me if I don't put out the fire, she'll douse my charcoal with her water bottle. I tell her, in my most gentlemanly voice, that a) I appreciate her concern but I'm the one eating the meat; b)would she like to mind her own business; and c) aren't those running shoes leather and did she think that cow died of natural causes.

"Unfortunately, this just adds fuel to the flame, so to speak. She issues an ultimatum - 'if I don't put the barbecue out, I'll have to use the steaks on the two black eyes she's going to give me.' I'm thinking - like hell, she'd have to stand on a stool to reach me. But I figure this woman's wacko and by now my domain has been totally invaded.

"I decide it's not worth continuing our discussion, so I put the barbecue out. None too soon, because by that time, several more people gathered carrying signs protesting meat-eaters. I wondered how they got there so fast? With signs - no less. Do you think they carry them around just in case they come across an opportunity to protest something? What's our country coming to?" George looked confused and hurt over the treatment he received. (Or maybe it was just early onset arteriosclerosis?)

I'd heard of things like this happening but George was the first person I knew to experience this kind of confrontation. Yes, we baby boomers were again standing up (albeit not quite so straight) for what we believed in, just like in the 60's and 70's. I was torn between feelings of hip, hip, hooray for the skinny woman and why don't people mind their own business?

I finally sided with George, seeing his distress in recalling the unseemly event. I knew how his pride must have suffered knuckling under to a mere woman. This was new territory for him.

I determined to get his mind off it. "George, maybe she forgot her Prozac that day. Speaking of drugs, what about them? Did anyone bring them in to get really into the moment of the original Woodstock? Yes, oh yes, good ol' LSD and THC."

"No. A, B, C, and DHEA though."

Glancing at my watch, I suddenly realized I was late for an interview I'd scheduled that morning before heading to the coffee house. "I've gotta go George. I've got an appointment. It's been great. Oh, you don't mind picking up the check, do you? My social security money hasn't arrived yet. And besides I have to rush home or I'll miss the folks from meals on wheels." I kidded.

Not giving George an opportunity to decline, I ran from the coffee house. After all, I'm just a poor author and George is making a bundle these days. The Beatles' tune "will you still need me, will you still feed me, when I'm 64?..." ran through my head.

II. Down the Up StairMaster

My butt's as big as a house!

The appointment I'd made that morning before my trip to the coffee house, was with a friend - Jennifer. I chose Jennifer because she's tall and slender and works out everyday as religiously as she attends her neighborhood New Age church. I thought she'd be an excellent candidate to begin research for my book. The day we talked she was huffing and puffing up an imaginary hill on her stationary bike. Just another boomer racing the clock.

"I'm writing a book about boomers' trials and tribulations of getting older. What do you have to say about that? You know, what's your perspective about this whole age thing?" Pretty succinctly put, I thought.

"Are you referring to the inter-generational sequential spiral of relational offspring, or the actuality of inter-dimensional relativity?"

(Gulp) "I'm talking about bulges. Crows-feet. Wrinkles. You know, the six-thirty-in-the-morning-look-in-the-mirror that makes you want to up-chuck. You begin to think you're the victim of some horribly twisted version of the Folger's coffee switch. You know, someone secretly replaced the young lithe and firm body of 'moi' with the softer, slightly sagging, wrinkled body of the middle-aged baby boomer."

Jennifer is on the StairMaster now. Light sweat is beading on her brow and upper lip. Her boyfriend enters the room...thirty-two, rippling muscles, looks like Charles Atlas. (Oops, there I go showing my age again. If I mention Charles Atlas to him, he'll probably ask if he's, perhaps, a cousin of Rand McNally.) "Whoa baby! You look better everyday. Catch you later on for some tennis." He grabs his jacket and is gone.

Jennifer smiles at me and asks, "What were you saying?" (Obviously a bad person to schedule my first appointment with.) Jennifer appears to be having absolutely no trials or tribulations, which further confirms my suspicions that baby boomers are in denial over the aging thing.

As I left Jennifer's condominium, I decided that I had at least determined the right angle to take my book even if I didn't have the right person. I thought about my options and got inspired. So I headed for the health club, out on the edge of town where all the yuppies live.

If there are any group of people representative of the baby boomer mentality, it's yuppies. Trouble is, the acronym no longer fits. The Young Upwardly Mobile Professionals are no longer young, many having become old, sarcastic, and tired.

Technically, the Yuppies were really younger than many of the baby boomers. But, the baby boomers, a group that know a good thing when they see it, jumped on the bandwagon. (Although some of us needed a little help up.) They liked the lifestyle, the BMW's, and the tight butts that went with being a Yuppie. They adopted Yuppiedom and made it their own.

Upon entering the club, I was immediately surrounded by sweating people. I picked out one, a virile looking guy who seemed about my age. (Though given my experience to date, he would probably deny it.) I approached him warily. My experiences with Jennifer and George had burned me.

"Hi. I'm writing a book about baby boomers and how they're reacting to growing older. Could you give me a little input?"

The large gold chain hanging on his hairy chest glistened sweatily. Drops of perspiration fell from his curly locks. This guy emanated sex and charm. Romance novel material for the gray-haired set. His eyes met mine. "Anything you want, babe. Ask away."

"Well, how do you feel about getting older?"

He flexed a corded arm. "Hey, I'm not getting older, I'm getting *better.* Never *felt* better in my life. Never *looked* better." He leered at me, his brown eyes glowing with health and lust. "Never *did* it better, either." He put a wet arm around my shoulders. "Want to come see my etchings?" He chuckled throatily. "I got some great ones."

I pulled back quickly. This definitely wasn't going where I wanted it to go. "Some other time. *I'll* call you." I beat a hasty retreat to the office for my buddy, Jim. Maybe I could get some straight info from him.

Jim's office is plush, desert pink and blue. Cacti made out of fabric sit on shelves. The music playing in the background reminds me of church when I was a kid...chanting. Now, very in, I understand. If those old monks had only known. They could have made a bundle, rather than living on bread and water.

Jim was talking with a lady, forty-five or so, and pretty

good looking. (I could tell her seven and a half seconds hadn't come and gone yet.) She left, and we sat down. Again, I explained my mission.

"Wow, did you come to the right place. Baby boomers are my mainstay. They're my reason for being in business. I love, let me emphasize - *love* - baby boomers."

"So what do you think drives them? (My guess…in a couple of years a home healthcare attendant.) What're their goals when they come to a place like this?"

Jim rolls his eyes. He's about thirty-five, and ruggedly handsome. He worked in construction, but found that there were bigger bucks in the body business. "Vanity. This is one group of people who just don't think they're ever going to get old. You know, the Pepsi generation. All previous generations have just moved along, accepting the changes that come with the territory. Not these folks. They've been fed a continuous line through television that they have to be and remain thin, sexy and beautiful. Trouble is, most of them aren't."

Being one of this crowd he's talking about, I digested that. "What's the story on Mr. Charming over there?" I asked, pointing at my would-be seducer wearing the Mr. T starter kit.

"Mike? Stays in pretty good shape for fifty-five. Course, he's taken a few turns with Doctor Facelift. Tries every new vitamin that comes down the pike. His insides must be coated with gelatin from all the pills. As for sex, it's more of a hold up than a stick up. He just got a penile implant last week. Works really good, I hear. He'll never grow old, just collapse on the StairMaster."

I was deflated. He'd looked so...so capable. Not my type, but still I like to think there's someone out there that can still...well, that's another topic. Any way, back to Jim.

"So, you think this whole exercise thing is just vanity? These people aren't really interested in being healthy, just sexy and beautiful?"

"That's my take on it. Except maybe Virginia over there." He nodded towards a heavy woman in a black and white warmup suit reminiscent of Shamu. She was working with a personal trainer and Latin God. I've seen freight trains puffing less going up mountain passes. "She's here five days a week. Works on every machine. Why don't you talk to her?"

I left his office and walked over to Virginia. "Hi. I'm writing a book on baby boomers and how they feel about getting older. Any comments?"

"Thanks...I need to rest a moment. Julio, give me ten minutes." Julio smiled, bowed slightly, and moved off to the fruit bar at the side of the room. He was dark, slender, and very tanned. Virginia's eyes followed him as he sat down next to a blonde, a very young blonde. Virginia, short, graying and dumpy, was still huffing as we climbed onto a couple of stationary bikes.

"It's all a farce. I come here everyday, exercise my ass off, and still look the same. Look at my butt. Big as a house." She sighed. I felt bad for her. Her butt definitely had not fallen.

It was too big to fall. If it did it would register on the Richter scale.

"So why do you do it?" I asked curiously. "Why not just sit home, eat Twinkies, and enjoy life?"

Another sigh. "My husband. The children. As long as I'm here, they think I'm trying. I've been on Weight Watchers for five years." She looked around furtively. "You promise you won't tell something if I confide in you?"

I wanted to shout, "Lady, I'm writing a book! Why do you think I'm asking you these questions?" Instead, I pulled closer and looked secretive. Writers have their faults, too.

"I'm a closet Dove Bar eater." (Ooh...there's a news flash. I'll alert the media. I'm guessing it's a walk-in closet.) "I can't resist them." She looked sad. "I eat fifteen, twenty a day." (An entire flock of Dove Bars.)

"Wow," I commented supportively, "that's about a million calories. Where do you eat all those so that no one will see you?"

She looked at me like I was a little slow on the uptake. "In the closet. Hellooooo... We've got this little room off our closet. It was designed to hide your stuff in. We don't have any "stuff" to hide. I spend all our extra money on Dove Bars and the gym. Anyway, I put this tiny little freezer in there, and keep it stuffed with Dove Bars. The only thing I worry about are the mice."

Now I was really confused. Last time I noticed, food in a freezer doesn't attract mice. I had to ask, even though I wasn't sure I wanted to know. "Uh, Virginia, I don't understand how food in a freezer can draw mice?"

This seemed to confirm her opinion of my intelligence level. She spoke as if to a small child. "The dripping from the Dove Bars. It's all over the place." She made a face. "Now, I've begun noticing mouse droppings in there. At first I thought it was chocolate. Wrong! How can I call an exterminator without telling my husband? It's just all getting so complicated," she whined.

"I see your point. How about just setting a trap?" From the expression on her face, I might have suggested feeding a few Christians to the lions. So apparently, she was willing to risk triggering adult onset diabetes - but kill a mouse? - parish the thought. What did she think the exterminator was going to do? Offer Mickey and Minnie a corporate relocation package? "Bad idea. Sorry, guess I can't help you with that one."

It was time to move on. "Good luck, Virginia. I'm sure this will all work itself out somehow." As I walked away, Julio was returning and Virginia was at it again, trudging up a treadmill toward thousands of beautiful Dove Bars.

Leaving the health club, I decided to drive through town. I'd noticed women out walking about noon, in dressy suits, nylons and Nikes. They looked very determined as they elbowed their way along the streets. I decided to drive by again and check it out. Yup. There they were. Walking as if their lives depended on it.

I decided to investigate. Why were they walking in their

suits? And nylons!? Did they walk quickly enough to work up a sweat? How did they smell when they returned to the office? Did their non-walking *co-workers* spend their afternoons humming…"a sprinkle a day…?"

The next day at noon found me nudging my way through the crowded sidewalks looking for one of these exercisers. I didn't have to go far. Actually, I didn't have to go anywhere. She almost bowled me over. A tall woman maybe five-foot-ten, about forty-five, brown hair and eyes. She wore a classy red tweed suit and Nike running shoes. "Sorry," she said out the corner of her mouth as she breezed by.

I walked faster to keep up with her swinging stride (which was no small feat for a five-foot two-inch person). "Hi. I'm writing a book about baby boomers and this aging thing. I was kind of focusing on the way they exercise and noticed you and a lot of other women walking around in your suits and Nikes at lunchtime. What gives?"

She was huffing slightly. "It's the only time I can exercise. And as an incentive, my company negotiated lower insurance rates for exercisers." We turned a corner in tandem, almost mowing down a little old lady using a walker, wearing Nikes. I guess you're never too old.

"Young whipper snappers!" disdain dripped from her lips as she shouted and waved her walker up and down in the air at us. I was impressed she could swing her walker that well. "No respect for your elders!" As we crossed the next street, I turned to see her still waving the walker. Maybe she was still mad, or maybe she was working her upper body.

I'm thinking - so the insurance companies are encouraging this lunchtime frolic, not at all concerned with air quality in the office, or the comfort of the exercisers' co-workers. How ironic. Smokers have been banned to the great outdoors, but B.O. is allowed. From this, I surmised that second-hand smoke must be more lethal than B.O. Having slowed down with my thoughts, I suddenly realized my walker was pulling away. I focused and fought to stay up with her as she continued her story.

"I have three teenage sons and a husband at home. I'm up at 5:30, fixing breakfast, and getting them off to work and school. My evenings are spent working on my avocation - painting. Eventually I hope to make a career out of it. I'm only working my current job to help support the family, and to pay for painting supplies and classes."

"How on earth do you find free time in the evenings with three teenagers?" I had one word for her - delegate.

"That's a good question. You know I used to pick up after them constantly. The weekends were spent doing 12 and 13 loads of laundry, cleaning bedrooms and bathrooms, while Randy, my husband, took the boys out to spend the day fishing, playing basketball, or some other fun thing. I got tired of the housework and of being stuck at home."

She continued. "That wasn't the worst of it though. I learned a long time ago, it's impossible to keep a teenager's bedroom clean, but I kept trying. The straw that broke the camel's back happened when I was cleaning one of their bedrooms. I found a hoard of magazines, clothes, and other unmentionable things under one of the beds. At the same moment, I spotted one of my good plates with, what looked like, a half eaten meal on it. I couldn't tell for sure because it was covered with green fur. I wondered if I needed to wash it or take it down to the river and set it free. When I got down on my hands and knees to fetch the plate, I saw two yellow eyes staring back at me."

"Your cat stays under the bed with all the stuff?" I assumed.

She came to an abrupt stop, turning to look me straight in the eye. (Of course, she had to bend over to do it.) "No! We don't *have* any pets!"

"Yikes! I see." Those bedrooms must be worse than even I could imagine. And I could imagine a real pigsty, having grown up with a brother. My brother even had a pet Water Moccasin until Mom found out it was poisonous. I'll never forget the fit she had about that one. My walker had begun walking again. "What'd you do?"

"Left the plate there. I didn't want to know what was lurking under the bed. That was the last straw. No more. I told them from then on keeping their rooms clean was their responsibility and if they wanted to sleep in a pigpen, fine."

"Good for you." I admired her courage, living in a house with who knows what kind of creatures lurking about.

"Yes. Well...it would have been great but I made the mistake of continuing to do their laundry. I wouldn't have minded so much, except when I went to collect it, the hamper was always empty. Now that I wasn't cleaning their rooms, I dreaded going in, but did it anyway, to pick up dirty clothes.

"Unfortunately, I couldn't tell the clean ones from the dirty ones, since the boys' bedroom floors now served as their closets. I'd pick up every piece of clothing and wash it. Week after week this went on. Finally it dawned on me, I must be washing clean clothes. Duh... Of course this added immensely to my joy. I kept thinking 'I'd rather be painting.' Finally...I'd had enough. Why should I be the one doing all the work when I represented only twenty percent of the household? That was the turning point. I decided right then and there - no more laundry! This woman's going to have a life!"

"That's wonderful. But what I think I'm hearing you say, is that your husband hasn't been much help."

"Help what? Get the house dirtier? Make a bigger dent in the sofa? Leave the toilet seat up? He helps alright. Just like he helped bring those three kids into the world. You have kids? No, I thought not. Don't let those sitcoms on TV fool you. Holding your hand in the delivery room and saying, 'count honey,' and 'push, honey' isn't the same as having that baby. Not by a long shot. Yeah. He helped. He took the kids out of the house on the weekends so they wouldn't get in the way of my cleaning."

"Sounds pretty tough." I commiserated.

"Probably not different from most women with children. But I wasn't going to lie down and take it. With laundry out of the way, my last obstacle to free time was cooking dinner every evening. Even though we didn't have a firm rule about everyone sitting down for supper like a civilized family, I was stuck with food preparation, and the boys appreciated it so much, they took theirs and sat in front of the TV, or went to their rooms. Of course this is what fed the creatures living under their beds." She shuddered. "And since I no longer entered their rooms, we rapidly ran out of dishes. 'No more,' I said. Now they have to cook for themselves, or Randy picks up take-out. Voila! Free time."

I could tell, *this* was an unusual woman. Many mothers catered to their children into adulthood. "How's Randy doing with your liberated woman approach?" Sounded like this was quite a transition for all of them.

"He groaned about it for the first three months, until he discovered that I actually had more time and energy for sex. Then he decided it wasn't such a bad deal. And, as an added bonus, we have his favorite dish, pizza, once a week. Of course, I couldn't eat pizza that often if it weren't for my lunch-time exercise ritual."

"I see. Well, thanks for all this great information. You certainly seem to know what you want out of life and aren't afraid to go after it."

"Thanks."

"Good luck with your painting." We parted company. I felt like I'd just met an incredible person. She was planning for a different future, readying herself. And, I now had some idea of how much focus and commitment it took to keep up with a full-time job, a part time avocation, and three teenage sons. Thank God I wasn't married!

I'm here my child. Always available. At your beck and call. Always here. You're the only one in the Universe that I have to attend to. The essence of Godliness. That's me.

I didn't mean for you to come. I was just musing about marriage and the disparity between what it requires of women. Apparently it takes two incomes to survive anymore and it seems to me that women get the short end of the straw. Not only do we receive disparate pay for equal jobs with men, but after work we come home and take care of children, cook, clean, and launder. Whew!! Like I said, I'm glad I'm not married.

Tell me, why *did* you invent marriage anyway? Weren't you happy giving us just *one* Lord and Master?

> It wasn't my idea. You're the ones who wanted to have sex and keep the population going!

You mean it wasn't you who said, "...until death do you part?"

> Nope.

Why do it then?

> Because you feel better about yourselves when you're experiencing a loving relationship. That's why you keep looking for that special person (or thing) to make you feel good. When you're in the presence of another's obvious affection, you blossom.

Problem is - you wither when they choose
not to focus on you.

So, you're saying we shouldn't get married?

No. I'm saying...you should love yourselves first.

III. To Eat Or
Not To Eat...

Why does it have to be so hard
to look good?

I was becoming aware of a recurring theme in the interviews, an almost maniacal compulsion to have a thin, trim, and ageless body. Looking back now into the not so distant past, I thought about such mega-stars as Marilyn Monroe, Gina Lollabrigida, and Jane Mansfield, none of whom were will'o'wisps by a long shot.

As far as I could see, the first really thin icon was Twiggy. For some unknown reason, she appealed to a generation that was growing up with the threat of nuclear war hanging over them. Maybe our little psyches were telling us to get used to having less food after the big bang. Or worse yet, it could have been the influence of growing up with pictures of skinny, huge-eyed little kids and kittens hanging on the wall over our beds. I immediately turned to God to get a straight answer on this.

                                                    ~

Well, God, only you can answer this one. Why are we so hung up on having these thin bodies?

> Taste in beauty has changed so many times in your world that I've given up trying to figure you out.

You continuously surprise me. You're God, right? Didn't you make Adam and Eve beautiful? After all, they were supposed to have been made in your image. Wouldn't God be the

---

Yikes!! My Butt's Falling

best looking person of all?

> And you continuously surprise me. I'm *an* essence. I'm *love.* I'm *consciousness. When are you going to get it?!!* I don't have a body to be ugly or beautiful. And there wasn't really an Adam or Eve. That's a story that some people made up to repeat when they were sitting around the camp-fire on cold nights in the cave. (Sigh) It's a good thing I *AM* God and have all the patience in the world.

Well, ***excuuuuuse me!*** I guess since you have all the patience in the world, you got some of mine.

> Forgive me. (Chuckle) Can't you take a little joke? Sometimes I forget that you humans aren't quite as evolved as...well, anyway, back to this body thing. See, a bunch of you (in non-physical form) came to me and wanted a new place to play. You said some-thing about being a little bit bored wearing wings. Give us a new toy, you said.

Give us a world where we can go to work on things, where we can try out new experiences, where we can ride the "El".

Sounded okay to me, so I set up a committee to design the place and lay down some ground rules. An eon or so later, the committee came back with a plan for this planet called Earth. Actually - it was some darn good work.

Of course, I had to do a little clean up on the whole thing, but basically I left it as it was in the original plan. Remember, I keep telling you, there's this free will thing. So I let you guys who wanted to go dinking around, have at it. All in all, I feel like it's been quite a success.

You mean to say that *you* didn't design all this, that we were thought up by some *committee*? No wonder we have so many problems. Sending something to a committee to be worked on is usually the worst thing that can happen to a project. All those egos.

Ah, but you forget, you wanted the challenges. That's the whole point of the exercise. And secondly, the non-physical world is different. Committees here do a darn good job. No egos. All is love. Anyway, variety sounded like such a nice concept. Thin, fat, good, bad, pretty, ugly. And everything in-between. We thought - "what a lovely set of contrasts,"

The free will bit was done as an afterthought. Since we have it in the non-physical form, everyone on the committee decided it should be part of the physical experience. Are you saying that it isn't working out well? I hadn't noticed that. No one in this realm has come to complain to me. You have to understand that once you're free of earthly physical form, you remember how this all happened, and don't take it seriously at all.

This is beginning to sound like earth is just a theme

park for bored non-physical entities. Sort of a Knotts Berry No Physical Form Farm. Tell me the truth now, is it?

Uhh, well...oh, I hear St. Peter calling... something about an emergency over in the Delta Quadrant...a worm hole collapsing or something...gotta beam up...live long and prosper.

Hmmmm…well, that was a bit of a revelation. Maybe we have been taking this whole life thing too seriously. Look at poor Virginia, slaving away at the gym during the day, sitting with other overweight women during the evening at some diet program, and in between, gorging on Dove Bars. I wonder what her 'non-physical entity' will think about this earthly experience after leaving the body. I really feel the need to get some other perspectives on this thing. Talking to God can be a little overwhelming.

I think I'll call my friend, Cheryl. She works on her figure constantly. Every time I see her, she's on some new diet - Beverly Hills, Atkins, the Zone, Protein Power, Plastic Packing Peanuts and Spackle. She seemed the perfect baby boomer to talk to about diets.

"Cheryl, how are you? Haven't seen you since your birthday party at the Hilton. Great party. What a neat husband, giving you a surprise bash and all."

"It was the best. I love the silver bracelet you gave me. Wear it all the time."

"Good. Listen, I'm writing a book on baby boomers, and of course dieting reared its ugly fat head. I thought you might have some stories to tell about the subject. I know you've tried them all."

"I certainly have. Listen, some of these diets can kill you. Look at that doctor from Scarsdale. Dead as a door nail."

"But Cheryl...wasn't he killed by a lover?"

"She may have pulled the trigger, but it was the diet that killed him. He got famous off the diet, and thinking he was hot stuff, played around on the girlfriend. See what I mean?"

This was a stretch for me, but somehow in Cheryl's mind it made sense. I wasn't going to argue. "Okay, I see your point. But, how many diets have you tried?"

"I actually counted them one day. Forty-three. I think the worst one was the cabbage soup diet. You make this cabbage soup, and eat it until you smell so bad they won't let you into a grocery store or a restaurant. You lose weight by default."

I grimaced. "Sounds pretty awful. Which one was the best?"

"Actually, none are that wonderful. The bottom line is, if you can't eat what you want to eat, life can be terrible. I just don't understand why it has to be so hard to look good."

I mumbled something about blaming it on the committee.

"What was that? A committee? Have they come up with a new diet? I thought that I'd done them all. I'll have to look that one up. Sounds interesting. Anyway, I'm starting the grapefruit diet tomorrow. Grapefruit three times a day, rice twice a day, and lettuce on the even days. Odd days you get steak."

"Sounds like a lot of acid to me," was my only comment.

"You're right. Fortunately, my body can take it. I'm very alkaline."

I wondered if I was too acid or too alkaline. Where *do* people find out these things?

"Anyway, I'd love to chat more, but I have to get to the store. They're having a sale on grapefruit, and I've got to stock up. I heard the weather wasn't too good in Florida, and prices are going through the roof. Bye!" And that was all from Cheryl. I was disappointed. I'd counted on her to be my diet guru. Now I had to work to find someone else. Who would it be?

The next morning I was at the coffee house again, stoking up on java. Suddenly I spotted Chris, my buddy who writes for a newspaper. He came over and sat down. Chris is at the young end of the baby boomer designation, and looks it. I didn't see how he could help me, but I was wrong.

"Chris, how you doin'?"

He shook his head. "Good, now that I'm home." He looked furtively around the small cafe. "Do you notice anything...I mean, do I...do I smell okay?"

"What's the matter? Have you been on a safari and got caught in an elephant litter box?"

He looked disgusted. You see, he does feature articles, and gets sent to these unique places to get weird stories. He also doesn't think I'm very funny.

"Yeah, right. No, I just got back from this health spa in Gilroy, California. The paper paid for my buddy and me to go and get the story. After this experience, I'm ready to go into some line of work that's easy. Like diffusing bombs. It was one of the worst experiences of my life. I would rather drive carpet tacks into my gums than do that again."

As usual, I was confused. Getting paid to go to a health spa sounded like a job I could get used to real easy. I said something to that effect.

"You don't understand. This spa puts you on a special diet. Thirty cloves of garlic a day. (Turns out Gilroy, California, is the garlic capital of the world with the Garlic Festival, Miss Kyolic, and the whole nine yards.) Oh, they dress it up, chopped up in salads, diced up in other vegetables, but it's all raw.

"Then there's the massage room. Two massages a day, with garlic oil. The hot tub has garlic essence in the water. The mud bath has garlic in it." He shook his head again at the memory. Now that I'd been sitting next to him for a moment, I was definitely catching an aroma. Thanking my lucky stars and secretly glad that I'm not a vampire, I quietly slid my chair a notch away from him.

"Wow," I said. "Now, that's weird. How'd you survive?" I knew that Chris was a meat and potatoes man all the way.

He laughed. "Well, by the third day we were starving, not to mention gagging on garlic. That night we went over the wall."

"Literally? I mean, you had to climb a wall to get out? Had they taken your car keys away?"

"We didn't have a car. We flew in, and they met us at the airport. They had this limo take us out to the spa. This place is very plush. Besides, they don't want you to get away. They lock the gate at night. So, we climbed over the wall and walked three miles down the road to a steakhouse. You can tell how desperate we were!

"When we finally got there, we almost passed out from the sweet smell of charcoal and meat. We limped in and waited for the maitre d' to seat us. Our mouths were salivating just at the *thought* of real food. Were *we* in for a shock. Or, should I say, everyone else was. Apparently the garlic smell had permeated our bodies, and we reeked. The maitre d' came up to us, opened his mouth to greet us, and immediately pulled out his handkerchief and gagged. He wouldn't even seat us. He escorted us outside while they made take-out. By then we didn't even care. It was food."

My eyes were starting to water a bit. I slid a little further away. "That's quite a story. Did you lose any weight?"

"Oh, yeah. Mostly from walking down to the steakhouse every night. After that first night, they just put our food out back, and we slid the money under the door. It worked for everyone. I've been back for two days, and I think I'm finally getting the garlic out of my system. What do you think?"

"No problem. I can't smell a thing." I'd finished my coffee. "I do have an appointment in the Delta Quadrant, though."

"What?"

"Sorry - inside joke. Take care." And I was gone. Somehow, I think I've lost my taste for garlic.

I walked out the door and immediately ran into an old business client from another life, Jane. We were going the same direction, so I started telling her about the book and my current research around dieting. At which point, she asked politely, if it somehow involved a large quantity of garlic? "No. That's a long story for another time." She was only too happy to comment for my book. She was even the right age.

"Everyone I know is on a special diet of some kind. I refuse to entertain anymore because of it."

This sounded promising. "Have you had some bad

experiences?" I asked.

"Well, let's put it this way. There's a group of women I run around with since Doug and I got divorced. We have lots of fun, and I hardly miss Doug. But I soon found out that women my age have lived long enough to develop beliefs around what they ingest. You know, 'you are what you eat'."

She ticked each of her friends off, one by one on her fingers. "Bev won't eat any kind of meat or dairy product. Angie will eat chicken, but not beef or pork. Betty is allergic to gluten, and can't eat anything made from wheat flour. Debbie will eat only free range chicken, raised the way God intended, and organic vegetables. Carol will only drink bottled water and eat food washed with bottled water. I only eat fat free foods. And Andrea...well, she'll eat positively anything, but then she probably swallows her index finger for dessert."

I could see that this would be an entertaining night-mare. "So how do you all handle this?"

"We do potluck most of the time. It's BYOO - Bring Your Own Obsession." She looked at the sidewalk in a most melancholy way. "I used to love to have dinner parties. You know, get out the good china and crystal, buy a crown roast, and make a really gooey chocolate dessert. People raved about

---

my cooking." She looked wistful. "That's all over now. Everyone is so health conscious that food is no fun anymore. My therapist says that I use food as a substitute for love. That may be true, but," and here she grinned wickedly, "you don't get hair in your mouth with chocolate."

My mouth may not have had a hair in it, but it certainly dropped open wide enough to dig anything out. Jane's audacity had definitely gotten to me. But then, she'd been an aggressive salesperson. "Jane, I wish you luck. Who knows, maybe you'll get married again. You're too attractive and too intelligent to stay single long."(As if those traits qualify anyone for marriage.)

She laughed contentedly. "Maybe. But I think I'm past the need for a man in my life. My therapist says that men are a metaphor for security. I just need a new security blanket. I'm taking up some new hobbies, trying to find myself. I'm going rollerblading Saturday. Want to come?"

Shades of the sixties, I thought. She's trying to find herself. "Thanks, but I like my parts where they are, all in one piece. See ya." I had just started the car when I realized that it was getting towards noon, and the coffee had only whetted my appetite.

Down the street I spied a chicken fast food restaurant that had just opened. Fast Food. We baby boomers had been weaned on fast food. Why, I could remember my first fifteen cent hamburger when I was just a little kid. What a great place to see if I can glean more insight into our eating habits.

When I opened the door, I was amazed to see Andrew, an old acquaintance. I was even more amazed to learn that he owned the place. You see, this was Chicks and Collards, a chain that specialized in southern fried chicken with all the trimmings. You know, greens, grits, mashed potatoes, and so on.

I remembered that Andrew was a died-in-the-wool vegetarian. So how was he justifying murdering all those feathered friends? As I approached him, he was standing over a family of five seated in a booth.

Andrew is a big guy, tall and powerful looking. He wore cowboy boots, jeans, a white blazer and a black bola tie. His eyes were closed and it seemed that he was praying, although his voice was booming. "Oh Lord, we thank you for this family and their good health." His voice raised a level. "We thank you for their patronage of our fine restaurant today."

His voice went up another level. "We thank you, oh

...And Lord, please send these fat calories to Africa...or whatever.

Lord, for taking these fat calories and sending them to someone who needs them. We know, oh Lord, that there are people in distant lands, Africa...or whatever, that have little to eat, and that right now you're sending them to where they can do the most good. And we thank you. Amen." The family was thanking him now, with a resounding chorus of 'bless you's', and he was moving off to another table that was waiting on him.

There was a replay, with slight variations, and then, as he scanned the room, he noticed me. I hated to tell him that I knew for a fact that God was, at this very moment, millions of light years away in the Delta Quadrant.

"Hello there!" He boomed. "Bless you my friend. Thanks for stopping in today."

"Sit down, Andrew. You can cut the Holy Roller crap for a minute, and chat with me. You *have* to tell me what's going on."

Andrew laughed, and became his old self as he sat down. "Hey, it's good to be able to relax. All this removal of fat is exhausting."

"Good gosh, Andrew, what happened? You were always the most committed vegetarian I knew. Now you're selling chicken?!"

He glanced around the room to make sure that no one was listening. "Yeah, I know it's weird. I don't quite understand it myself. It started about two years ago. I was visiting family in Louisiana. A major hunger attached struck while I was driving down the road and I spotted this Chicks and Collards restaurant. All of a sudden I had this overwhelming urge to pull in. It was like something out of The Twilight Zone, with my head saying one thing and my stomach another. I hadn't eaten chicken in probably ten years, hadn't even had the desire for *any* kind of meat in all that time.

"I drove around the place for what seemed like twenty minutes, hoping the feeling would go away. Besides, I was afraid the relatives might see me. They all think I'm a little strange anyway, being the only vegetarian in the family. I sure didn't want any of them to see me anywhere near meat.

Finally, though, I couldn't stand it any longer, and went inside. I found myself getting three orders of chicken, eating every bite, and even sucking on the bones..."

"I get the picture."

"Nothing ever tasted so good in my life. I was sure that I was under some dark spell by a warlock, don't sneer, I know a couple, and went to a cleansing ceremony at the Zen Temple when I got back here. But, it didn't work. I finally just gave in, and bought the darn franchise. Now I can have chicken anytime I want."

Wow, that's a story. *Vegetarian Relents and Chews a Chunk of Chicken.* "Okay, I can buy all of that. But what's all this prayer hocus pocus? Sending fat calories out to Africa? Andrew, have you flipped?"

He tried to keep the grin off his face, but couldn't make it. "Gees, I know it's even crazier than the other story. You know how all these baby boomers are, they want to be healthy, trim and slim. And I'm trying to sell them fried chicken and gravy. I wrote off for one of those mail order reverendships and hung it on the wall.

"Whenever anyone asks about the fat content, I just explain that I can 'pray away' the fat calories. Can you believe they swallow it? Pardon the pun. That shows how badly people want to eat fatty foods, but not get fat. As long as they pay, I'll pray." He looked like the cat that ate the canary. Or, should I say, that swallowed the greasy fried chicken.

I got an order to go, and as I left, I spotted Andrew praying with a mother and her two teenage daughters. From the size of their thighs, it looked like they needed an entire prayer meeting.

I'd heard enough about the baby boomers and our eating habits. It was time to move on to something really interesting - plastic surgery. The big nip, suck, tuck, and pluck.

IV. Plastic Splurgery

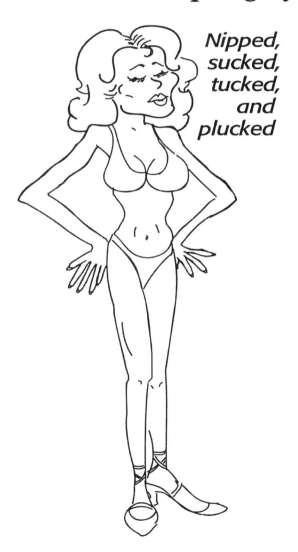

*Nipped,
sucked,
tucked,
and
plucked*

I headed back to the coffee house to gather my thoughts. Luckily, I was able to get my favorite table. I had a 2:00 p.m. appointment with Melissa but had time to stop by my apartment to chow on chicken and to hose off the garlic smell left from Chris. I was surprised that I'd arrived early enough to unwind. As I sat there sipping a low calorie cool mocha (now that sounds like an oxymoron), I considered how enlightening my research had been so far. It was becoming obvious to me that most baby boomers were concerned with their looks and chasing the fountain of eternal youth.

But what did I expect? We've been brainwashed into believing that it actually exists, having grown up on TV commercials and magazine ads. To top it off, we've observed people like Goldie Hawn, Cher, and Racquel Welch, who appear ageless. (Thanks in no small part to air brushing and camera lens filters.) Not wanting to get too philosophical, I returned to the present. Good timing, because in pops Melissa just in time for our appointment. I watch as she strolls over to my table. "Hey - Melissa. How are you?"

"I'm doing great. So why did you call this meeting?" She plops down in the chair across from me.

Melissa isn't plain, but she's not drop dead gorgeous either. She's always smiling as if she doesn't have a care in the world. I've known her for a couple of years through Jennifer, and I thought she would be a good addition to my research. "I'm writing a book on how baby boomers are aging. I thought you might give me some insights. You know...I talked to

Jennifer. Mistake! She's not aging."

Laughing, Melissa said. "You're sure clueless for a writer. I thought writers did their research? If you had, you'd know that silicone and collagen don't age."

"What are you talking about?" I'm feeling a little flustered, like Melissa is making fun of me.

Melissa's smiling like a Cheshire cat now. "Oh you silly. Jennifer had her fanny done, and rather than the end, it was only the beginning."

"What do you *mean*...she's had her fanny done?!" This meeting may end up being more fun than I anticipated, as well as providing useful information.

Melissa was giving me the look, the one Virginia had given me at the health club when I couldn't make sense of what she was talking about. The look that says - 'Gee, you're stupid.' I sat there waiting...and looking stupid.

Finally Melissa opens up, speaking in a hushed tone, afraid someone might overhear her, she whispers, "You know. She had plastic surgery to reduce and lift it." Now it's my turn to think - stupid you!! - I mean, I'm going to broadcast this tidbit of information to whomever is lucky enough to read my book.

"No! Are you sure? She's been very slim ever since I've known her." Hopefully, Melissa will spill her guts about Jennifer's little butt tuck.

"It's been over five years, but she definitely had her buns bobbed. A nip, suck, and tuck and she was riding high -

if you get my drift." Melissa, proud of coming up with such a colorful explanation of Jennifer's delicate derriere dilemma, puffed up a bit.

"Thanks for the insight. I always thought Jennifer was one of those fortunate ones born with great buns."

"Well, I guess she was until she developed duck butt. It migrated south." Melissa launched into more vivid details of Jennifer's trip to silicone valley. She'd whetted my appetite for more and I wondered why I hadn't thought of calling my friend, Patrick, the plastic surgeon, earlier. About ten minutes later, Melissa jumped up, exclaiming she was late for a hair appointment with Jon-Pierre, the hair specialist for the wealthy nipped, sucked, tucked, and plucked set.

I headed home. Once there, I rang up Patrick, a dear friend. There were hundreds of thousands of baby boomers undergoing plastic surgery and he could definitely share some stories. Anonymously, of course. Patrick was on the golf course but his nurse promised he'd call back just as soon as he finished.

I didn't have long to wait. The phone rang about thirty minutes later. It was Patrick. I explained what I was up to and Patrick, eager to share some of his stories, began talking the moment I stopped to take a breath.

"...this female patient of mine has come in for liposuction so many times, I have to use both hands to keep track. She seems to have an addiction to Dove Bars. Anyway, I tell her to lay off of them and she'd start seeing some results.

After all, she's at the health spa every day giving some semblance of working out. Between that and the liposuction, I swear she's probably lost 50 pounds of pure fat, several times over. Too bad we can't put that fat to use."

I couldn't believe my ears. He must be talking about Virginia. Surely there weren't that many women addicted to Dove Bars, yet also committed to attending the health club. "How interesting…" I barely got a word in edgewise.

"… ha, ha, ha. Isn't that a good one? Anyway, at this plastic surgeons convention, we shared some stories that'd make your toes curl, the best and worst facelifts. One of my colleagues was performing a redo. Seems someone had botched the job - in a big way."

Patrick's voice lowered to a conspiratorial tone. "This woman's eyes were pulled up so tight, she couldn't begin to blink, let alone close her eyes to sleep. She looked like a deer caught in the headlights of an oncoming car. And you should have seen her mouth, she wore a perpetual grin. My colleague was going to borrow some skin from somewhere else to loosen everything up a bit. Yup. Pretty soon this gal will be sporting some butt skin on her face." He added smugly, "Yeah, we see botched jobs every so often. Of course we don't speak about those with outsiders."

"Why do people take such risks with their faces?" I asked, wondering if looking young was worth the discomfort and possible disfigurement?

Patrick's voice held a sad note. "You know why.

Because they believe the advertising. Many of the people I see are just plain unhappy with themselves and think changing their looks will make a difference. It doesn't." Then, perking up, Patrick said his farewells. "Gotta go. I'm meeting a friend for a drink. He owes me."

"Thanks for your thoughts." Interesting. Now my mind was racing. I needed to interview someone who'd undergone some kind of plastic surgery to get another perspective. Sarah! Of course! She'd had a boob job. I rummaged around through my address book and found her number. I called right then. No reason to put it off.

"Hello?"

"Sarah, it's me. I'm writing a book on how baby boomers are aging and want to do a chapter on plastic surgery. I remembered you had your boobs enlarged. Are you willing to share that experience with my readers?" Sarah is pretty straightforward so I figured she would be a good sport about this opportunity.

"Sure. What do you need to know?"

"Just tell me about the surgery and share your thoughts around the decision making process."

"Well…it seemed to me that I was *too* flat chested. Guys simply weren't paying any attention to me. Every time I was out with a big-busted friend, you know - like Jennifer, they'd ogle her, treating me like I was the invisible woman."

Aghast, "But Sarah, do you really care about guys who're only interested in your bod?" I believed Sarah to be more substantial than this.

"You're right, of course. But I figured it wouldn't hurt to have a *little* something going my way. Anyway, I went to an excellent plastic surgeon recommended by Jennifer, who said he was recommended to her by a friend. This guy was marvelous, spending lots of time with me, showing me the implant and describing the surgery. He didn't miss a beat, except for one little detail." Sarah paused for effect.

"Come on Sarah. What little detail did he leave out?" I was becoming irritated at Sarah's dramatics.

"I'll simply say this - never let a male doctor determine the size of your implants."

"Enough said." I visualized Sarah walking bent over and weighed down with the large bosom she'd received under the hands of her talented and skilled surgeon. "Thanks. You've given me some good information. One more thing. Are you happy with the surgery?"

"Are you kidding? The guys stop on the sidewalks and gawk at me as I walk by. It's such a powerful feeling. To have so much control over another person that they have to turn for a second look."

This was getting to be too much. Though Sarah is straightforward, this was a little bit more truth than I cared to hear. "Thanks again. And good luck with those things."

I grabbed my bag and headed out the door for the beauty shop and Jon-Pierre. About a block away, I ran into Patrick's (the plastic surgeon) wife, Vicky. She always looked as if she

With these I have power over men!

stepped out of *Vogue* magazine. (Well, so would I if I were married to a plastic surgeon.) Today was no exception. Definitely a model-type. "Vicky, where you heading?"

"Hi! I'm on my way to Jon-Pierre's for my monthly trim. You know, he's a fantastic hairdresser. I wouldn't think of going to anyone else."

"I heard he's great. I can't afford to use him right now (maybe after this book sells 100,000 copies). I'm on my way to his shop to interview him for a new book I'm working on. I'll walk with you." This was a bit intimidating, walking with someone so attractive. Guys' eyes would bug out as she passed by. I remembered Sarah's comment about the feeling of power and wondered whether Vicky enjoyed that feeling too. I also noticed Vicky didn't pick up on my comment about writing a new book. Attractive *and* self-absorbed - what a great combination!

Vicky chatted happily about her marriage to Patrick and all the lovely parties they attended at the country club. This really wasn't my league. Partying at the country club was the last thing on my list of 1,000 terrific things I wanted to do with my life before I died.

We arrived at Jon-Pierre's in short order. The receptionist literally gushed over Vicky, while I stood there basically invisible. "How are you my dear? It's always a pleasure to see you. My, you're lovely as ever. I don't know why you're here, it's obvious you don't need our service..." and on and on. I thought I might gag.

Vicky was whisked off for her shampoo, giving Jon-Pierre a few moments to visit with me. We walked back to his plush office. Jon-Pierre was an attractive man, decked out in the latest leather garb, a pair of trousers and vest open to his waist. A gold chain draped his neck, laying against his tanned, smoothly glistening chest. (I wondered if he shaved it.) A gold ring and bracelet graced his hairless hand. Gold and diamond earrings (about ten) decorated his left ear. Good, I thought. Not *too* much jewelry.

His hair was dyed silver (to match the diamonds, I suppose) and gelled to stand up on top. Eyeing me appreciatively, Jon-Pierre motioned to a chair. I don't know whether his thought was that I might be fairly attractive or he simply coveted my outfit.

Jon-Pierre sat down in his teal blue leather chair behind a contemporary glass desk. Something about him reminded me of a fencer about to thrust, although I don't think I'd be his choice of fencing partner. "So, you mentioned on the phone that you're doing research on how baby boomers are handling the aging thing. I've only got a few moments right now. We're extremely busy today." He leaned back obviously enjoying his self-importance.

I parried. "I won't take much of your time." Kissing ass is my forte. "I know you're the hairdresser to the stars in this town and I just knew you'd have some juicy stories." I figured a few pats on his tush might help him spill his guts about his famous clientele. Anonymously, of course.

Jon-Pierre puffed up a bit more, if that was possible. "Well...you're right, we do cater to some pretty influential people here and confidentiality is crucial. You're well aware that hairdressers are in the know. *Particularly* me. I'm aware of every aspect of my clients' personal lives or I wouldn't be able to create an absolutely perfect ambiance for them. After all, hair and make-up, you know, is the stage setting for the personality. *In fact*, my clients are more intimate with me, than with their spouses." Jon-Pierre gloated.

I watched in awe. He wasn't simply puffed up, but down right pompous. Jon-Pierre was not fencing now. I had success-fully pierced his business shell and the ego underneath was blossoming. Kind of like that giant hybrid plant in *The Little Shop of Horrors.*

"For instance," and he leaned across his desk girlishly, "the woman you walked in with has had so much surgery, her face is filled with silicone. Her eyebrows have been tattooed on. Her nose has been pugged and perked. Her jaw line rounded and firmed." His face took on a tortured look. "You wouldn't believe what I go through to style her hair in such a way as to hide the scars, even though they're minor." he anguished. I almost believed he cared. But a second later, fixing me with his steel-blue eyes, "Of course, you mustn't let anyone know where you heard that little tidbit."

Surprise thrust. Ah...in the end, he'd outmaneuvered me. I assured him our conversation wouldn't go any further. (At least, *not in exactly* the same way he related it. I promised myself that *my* thrust would be the last and the sweetest.) "Why do you suppose people go through so much to look beautiful?"

He stroked his silver hair. "They're looking for love. That's why *so many* come to me. I give them what they want, my full attention and loving pampering. I treat them as if *they* are the ones that are queens. They feel like a million dollars when they leave here. And I make a million bucks giving them what they want." He gave me his most beguiling smile. "Now, if you'll excuse me. I must return to my darling clients." (Pigeons more likely.)

"Certainly. Thank you for your enlightening comments." As I walked out of Jon-Pierre's office into the lavish beauty

---

shop, I passed Vicky and others being polished, pasted, pampered and pummeled. I felt like a mongrel among elegant purebreds. I wondered whether, after selling a million copies of this book, I'd find plastic surgery and pampering, appealing. Who knows?

I strolled home, considering what I'd heard. Poor Vicky. Was Vicky going to Jon-Pierre because she didn't feel loved? Why didn't she feel loved? Did the plastic surgery help? Or was this just a change of life thing? I determined to find out.

      ↾   ↾   ↾   ↾   ↾   ↾

I haven't talked with God since page 56 - it's probably time to check in with him.

I'm here.

You've been very quiet the last twenty-six pages. I was beginning to think maybe our conversations were merely a figment of my very fertile and creative imagination.

Nope. I'm really here. Humans think I'm loud, (after all I do take up a lot of space) like the giant in Jack and the Beanstalk. Truth is...I have a very still, small voice.

V. Hormonal Hell

One of the biggest hurdles the baby boomers are having to get over is that middle years thing, the change of life. For years it was urban legend that any man with any balls at all would hit the change of life with a bang. This usually manifested itself as having an affair with that cute secretary, buying a sports car, growing his hair long or having a toupee made.

As this was all pretty straightforward and predictable, the average with-it wife could simply start watching for the first signs (anything from changing from boxer shorts to tiger-striped briefs, to making statements like, "We really don't need this stationwagon now that the kids are teenagers, do we?") and head it off at the pass.

This process has seemed to change somewhat, perhaps because so many women learned the ropes, took it in stride, and rolled with the punches. In short, some of these women said, "So long, Shorty," (not referring to any body parts you understand), dyed their hair, went to a spa, and ended up on a beach in France with some guy name Pierre who really appreciated a woman with 'ze expeerieence'.

Yes, the focus has shifted to the women and the fact that they really have a big hurdle to get over when they arrive at those 'certain years'. Menopause. It's a word that used to be shunned, spoken about in whispers, and the less said, the better. Just like PMS, men laughed about it when they got together in bars or on the golf course, assuming a holier-than-thou attitude of long sufferance of these female problems *they* had to endure.

You notice, I said, that men had to endure. The hot flashes, night sweats, and mood swings were viewed as major inconveniences for men, and women were expected to hold their suffering to a minimum for that reason. But, then came the baby boomers. These women are a new breed of human. They have the audacity to feel equal to men. Big change, after thousands of years of subjugation. Hmmmm...maybe I need to talk to God about this...

Well, God, I feel the need to talk again.

I'm always here, my child.

Tell me - did you inflict menopause on women because of the Garden of Eden incident?

How many times do I have to tell you that "Adam and Eve" story is simply that - a story.

I'm not sure I buy that one. I'm thinking that the change of life is a curse for suckering Adam into eating from the tree of knowledge. And I have to tell you, I've heard a new interpretation of that whole "Garden of Eden" story.

This should be good for a laugh. The other one certainly was. I mean, I'm omnipresent and I can't find Adam and Eve after they've eaten from the tree of knowledge? Explain that one.

Remember, supposedly they were hiding from you. Besides, we're getting side-tracked here. Do you want to hear this new version or not?

Lay it on me!

It's my understanding Adam, not Eve, had that eye-opening conversation with the snake, I think they called him Slider. Slider convinced that weenie, Adam, that living in the Garden was too namby-pamby. If he wanted to know what nudity was really about, he'd better eat the apple. Well, needless to say, Adam, being easily swayed by any authority figure, followed Slider right over to the tree encircled by an electric fence.

Warning signs were posted all over the fence, stating in huge letters "Off Limits to Humans." Of course the sign was wasted since Adam wasn't yet literate. At Slider's insistence, Adam straightened from his normal stooped position and flung himself through the electric fence, singeing his back hair, giving himself the first ever, electrolysis experience.

Once inside, he lifted a long dangling arm and plucked the choicest piece of fruit he could reach. Though he was naive, he wasn't stupid. Well...not that stupid. Rather than be the first one to taste this sweet morsel, he hulked back to find Eve.

She was by the stream, washing fig leaves, and contemplating the meaning of life. Adam, trying to get Eve's attention, jumped up and down, grunted, and did back-flips. (It seems that men have always preferred to communicate with us through their antics rather than with their words.)

Eventually Eve drifted over. Adam held out his furry paw, opened it right under Eve's dainty nose, and proudly displayed the shinny, bright red apple. Eve didn't lurch at the chance to eat the apple, though she did fall backwards trying to get away from the stench of Adam's fifthy paw. Apparently, bathing wasn't in his gene pool.

Adam, not to be put off, proceeded to make slurping noises and eating gestures. Finally to get Adam out of her face, Eve gave in and took the apple from his hairy and encrusted with "god knows what"...paw, and bit into it. To Adam's surprise, Eve fell over in a deep sleep, as if she were dead.

Wait a minute! That sounds like Snow White and the Seven Dwarfs.

You know - that's what I thought when I heard it. Are you suggesting that Disney stole his story-line from Adam and Eve?

No, I'd say Disney stole it from Grimm, who

stole it from Adam and Eve.

Oh…Wait a minute! We're getting off track. You're evading the question. Why do women go through the change of life and men don't seem to?

Same reason men don't get pregnant, they couldn't stand the pain. And that penile delivery would be a killer. Can you imagine men tolerating emotional up-heavals, hot flashes, dowager's humps, loss of sexual desire, expanding fannies, hair growing on their faces - I guess hair does grow on their faces - anyway, can you imagine what life would be like?

Yeah…it'd be hell.

Hey! Not a bad idea. I wish I'd thought of it.

Well - thank you for your insights. I couldn't have come up with them without you.

Any time. I'm always here for you.

ॐ   ॐ   ॐ   ॐ   ॐ   ॐ

So, I started out once again, seeking answers. Fresh

from this talk with God, it occurred to me that I could talk to my minister, Brenda. So, I called her up.

"Hey Brenda, it's me. I'm writing this book about baby boomers. This part is about the trials and tribulations of menopause. In other words - hormonal hell. Any comments?"

"(Deep sigh) It's a hard world. Though my ministry doesn't believe in a literal hell, *I've* certainly been experiencing one lately. I've been having all these mood swings. One day I'm feeling lower than a snake's belly in a wheel rut. I can hardly climb out of bed. I haven't got the energy to read a book much less write one, and as for a sermon, how can I tell someone else how to live their life when I'm not even sure I want to go on with my own? I feel like the lowest form of life on the planet. I run screaming in fear from singled-celled animals.

"Sounds terrible," I commiserated. "Have you gone to the doctor?"

"Yup. He said he figured that it was my hormones out of whack due to the change of life. After a bunch of tests and two weeks of pins and needles, he called me back. Thank goodness, he confirmed our suspicions. It's my hormones. This certainly took a load off my mind because I'd become extremely concerned that maybe I was really just a bitch."

"So what're you going to do about it?"

"I'm not sure yet, still investigating all the options. But the first thing I'm going to take care of is this mustache. (As I reflected on the last time I saw her, I realized she was beginning to look like one of the Mario Brothers.) The hairs above

---

my lip keep coming in thicker and stiffer every day. It reminds me of when I was little and spotted this woman in church sporting a dark brown mustache. Fascinated, I pointed my pudgy little index finger at her, yanked on my aunt's dress, and in loud tones said, 'Look at her! She has a moustache!' Embarrassed, my aunt stared down at me, an exasperated look on her face, 'Sssh, we don't talk about things like that.' At that precise moment, I promised myself I would never have a mustache, at least not one that showed."

"I certainly understand your frustration. Fortunately, I haven't experienced that problem. Are you going to go for electrolysis?"

"Honey - no! Tried it. Do you know how it feels to have every hair above your lip zapped with an electric current, then tweezed?"

"Ow...sounds painful."

"Painful? It hurts like hell! Plus you have the overwhelming feeling of wanting to sneeze when they get into that sensitive area right under your nose. Of course, anything's better than walking around looking like Saddam Hussein."

"I had no idea. Was there a problem with simply sneezing when the practitioner got into that sensitive area?"

"It's obvious to me you haven't experienced electrolysis or you'd know - it's pretty difficult to sneeze when you're prone on a table with a magnifying glass three inches away from your face, and an electric needle stuck up a hair follicle."

"That does sound a little tricky. So what I hear you

---

saying is that after undergoing all that pain, it wasn't even successful."

"Yup, and I spent over a year in this self-inflicted torture, not to mention a lot of money. Next I tried waxing. It worked great, and I only had to do it every few months.

"I thought I was back on track, my mustache problem conquered. But if it's not one thing, it's another. I began to notice little lines around my eyes, so I decided to try Retin-A. It worked great on the lines. But, if you haven't used it, you need to know that it causes your skin to become thinner and more sensitive.

"A couple of months into using the Retin-A, I went to wax my mustache. Mistake! I yanked off the strip of wax and, lo and behold, there, in the wax among those fuzzy little hairs, was a couple layers of skin. I damn near yanked off my entire upper lip! I looked like Robert Schuller!"

"Ouch!"

"Yeah. Make-up didn't cover it up. That was the end of waxing. Besides it wasn't exactly the way I'd envisioned having my face peeled."

"You're making me feel pretty lucky about my relative ease with my hormones and a nude upper lip."

"You know…when it rains, it pours. The menopause thing explains a lot about what's happening to me lately. For instance, the other day I was assessing my expanding figure in the mirror and noticed what I think is the beginning of a dowager's hump. I'm beginning to feel like the Hunchback of

Notre Dame."

"Whoa - no kidding? But doesn't that happen when you're older? You know - in your nineties?"

"Evidently not! When I noticed this hump, my entire world changed. Rather than seeing myself in 'hip' clothing, I now saw myself in broomstick skirts, over-sized shirts, sitting in a rocking chair crocheting, while my cat, Sid, batted a ball of yarn around the room."

"Come now. It's not that bad! Remember what you decided, 'the good news was that you weren't a bitch!'"

"You're right. I'm painting rather a bleak picture which doesn't fit into the positive, upbeat religion I preach every Sunday. You know, I was glad the doctor confirmed that my symptoms were caused by hormonal hell, because my ex-husband definitely believed I was a bitch, even offering to write a book about it. Maybe he was right. It was quite a ride before we split up, me starting menopause and him going through his mid-life crisis."

"I missed this story. Guess I need to come to church more often. Tell me what happened."

"Things were fine for five or six years. I wasn't a minister then, you know, and had to find my ecstasy with men, not God. Thank heaven that's over! Anyway, Bill and I were making those romance novels look like kindergarten stuff. Yup, it was pretty heady, knowing that we could teach the writers of the Kama Sutra a thing or two.

"But, I started growing as a person, getting spirituality and all, and the relationship just wouldn't take it. Bill talked a good game, but things started to change little-by-little. There was the time that the airline called, checking on the airline ticket for a certain little lady for a certain business trip Bill was taking. He really tried to weasel out of that one, telling me she was going to the French Riviera with him on business. I ask you, what kind of business does a dentist do on the French Riviera?" (I'm thinking drilling, but didn't say it.)

I couldn't help but smile at the naivete of men. "I see what you mean. Good ol' Bill wasn't exactly using his bean, was he?"

"Not by a long shot. Finally I hired a detective when he was going to a 'doctors only' conference in Miami. No families allowed, because they wanted the doctors to concentrate on the seminars without distractions. Or, so Bill said. Anyway...how's that for a line? The detective came back with pictures of Bill wrapped like a pretzel around this bleached-blonde-butt-lifted-breast-enhanced excuse for a female.

"Forgive me if I sound uncharitable. I'm sure she's a very nice person and I behold the Christ in her.

"You should have seen the look on his face when he saw those pictures. Turned right around and accused me of having them doctored. I was so mad I hit him right where it hurt most, in his sex life. The idiot had sent her flowers so I was able to find out her name from some credit card receipts. I was having one of my mood swings and was high as a kite when I called her up.

"I thanked her for taking ol' Bill off my hands, as he wasn't staying on his lithium very well any more, had charged up all the credit cards to the max, was wearing my clothes and not having them cleaned. Maybe he was even considering a sex change operation.

"I told her we were going to declare bankruptcy soon, and the kids and I'd keep the house so she could have him free and clear. I guess he'd been spending quite a bit of money on her, because it was obvious this hit hard. I added that he hadn't had any of his fits where he tried to kill me in my sleep for a while, and the doctors were hopeful.

"I positively dripped concern for how they were going to get by, now that he wouldn't have my parents to borrow from. I never enjoyed a phone call so much in my life."

"I can hear the satisfaction in your voice. I guess that broke them up for good."

"Yes, as a matter of fact she moved to another town and didn't even leave a forwarding address. Bill never did figure the whole thing out. Next day, the kids and I were gone too."

"So you blame this whole thing on your wild hormonal ride?"

She mused a moment. "That, and my growing up. But, maybe that's what happens. Women hit the change and, like a butterfly, come out of their cocoon. Men have a mid-life crisis and turn into moths."

"Interesting concept. Thanks for the info. See you in church."

Yikes!! My Butt's Falling

VI. Tick, Tock - Baby Begot

Hanging up the phone, I pondered Brenda's last comment as I headed out the door for the coffee house. Talking to Brenda was a bit of a bummer and I marveled again at how fortunate I was not to have so many of the problems many of my friends were experiencing around the menopause issue.

Once in the coffee house, I headed for the choice table next to the window. Fortunately it was available. I loved to sit there, sip a cappuccino and ponder the heart rending issues of aging I'd discovered were bothering baby boomers. Deep in thought, an old acquaintance, Sally, startled me when she suddenly appeared.

"Hi. It's been awhile. How've you been?" she asked, pulling out a chair and making herself at home.

At first a little perturbed with this interruption, my attention quickly diverted to her burgeoning belly. Obviously, quite pregnant, (although I didn't mention it. I've made *that* mistake before, "Are you expecting?") I decided to welcome her intrusion thinking she may have something to offer for my book. After all, lots of baby boomers were starting families in their mid-forties and I was curious about this enigma. Since Sally must be at least forty-four, I thought she could shed some light on it. "Sally, it's nice to see you. Let's catch up. I hear you're married."

"Yes - finally. I thought I'd made a mistake putting my career ahead of a personal life, but now I realize everything was in perfect order. My husband, Tom, is quite a catch. He's tall and muscular, with green eyes and blonde hair. A handsome blue collar type - all the rage. I finally met him when I took my car to his garage." Sally gloated ecstatically.

"You were spending so much time working - how'd you find time to meet him?"

"Oh it's quite a story. My friends were taking their cars to this certain mechanic. The word was - not only was this guy great with their cars, he was a feast for the eyes. My girlfriends would go on and on, telling me how he really cared about their cars and worked very hard to create a safe and loving environment in which they could share all their concerns." (This sounded familiar...oh yeah...Jon-Pierre! Maybe he had another business besides his salon.)

I snapped out of my trance long enough to let Sally know I was listening. "About their cars, of course."

"Yes! Anyway - it was time for my car's tune-up so naturally I took it to him. Honestly, the talk about Tom's drop-dead good looks was mind-boggling, so I just had to find out for myself. Was I surprised to discover the stories were greatly understated, at least to my way of thinking. And, my girlfriends were right. I'd never had anyone pay so much attention to my motor, lovingly listening to it's purr."

"You're speaking of your car - right?"

"Yes! Anyway, we hit it off and I asked him if he'd like to have dinner. He said yes, and as you can see, the rest is history."

"So, you're genuinely happy and looking forward to having a child? I didn't think you wanted to have children."

"Oh yes. Well you see, Tom is a few years younger than me and he definitely wanted a family. I felt that would be a small sacrifice to be married to such a loving and attractive (shallow) person."

"When are you due?"

"This is my third trimester. Actually, I'm due any day now. The baby's dropped to the birthing position and I've dilated three centimeters."

"Sounds to me like you should be in the hospital. How far do you have to dilate before the baby is ready to be born?"

"I'm not certain. But lately, I've had visions of the baby falling out on his little head."

"Don't worry, it'll never happen. I've heard it's hard enough to get them out when you're *fully* dilated. So, tell me. You're all right with being the mother of a teenager when you're in your 60's?"

"No problem. After all, many people are parents during middle-age."

I could tell from Sally's comment, she had definitely(?) thought this one through. This surprised me, because she was an extremely successful businessperson. I guess you can be a savvy businessperson and not too swift in other areas of your life. "Do you know whether it's a boy or a girl?"

"Oh yes! It's a boy! We saw his little thing-a-ma-bob on

the screen during ultrasound. Tom's so excited. He's already purchased a baseball glove, ball, bat and even a football. I reminded him that books are a good thing."

"What'd he say to that?"

"He said - 'only girls read books.' This is definitely an area we're going to have to discuss. Tom will be a good father though. He just loves children. You know he already has three from his first marriage."

"I didn't realize he'd been married before." I had the definite feeling that Sally may be destined for a shorter-term relationship than she'd desired.

"Yes. But only twice. They simply didn't work out. His ex-wives didn't understand how much he loves his work. Since I've been deeply involved in my own career, I have a much stronger aptitude for understanding. It doesn't bother me that he's at the shop by 7:00 a.m., and sometimes doesn't get home until well after midnight."

"Does he work all those hours?"

"Oh yes. He's just so fond of his clients." Furrows appeared in Sally's brow as she shared her deepest thoughts. "You know, he's about the most sensitive, sincere man I've ever met. I can certainly understand why his clients love him so much." (I'm picturing one of them up on the rack getting a lube at this very moment.)

"You're right. It's not too often that we meet such sensitive men as that." I commented tongue in cheek. "You're very fortunate."

This conversation was getting to be too much and really, I had all the information I needed. "Hey Sally, I'm writing a book on baby boomers and aging. Do you mind if I use some of your insights in my book?"

"How exciting! I'd love for you to." Sally's eyes widened. "But what insights did I provide?"

"Oh, you've been most helpful. I need to run now. It's been wonderful seeing you again. Good luck with motherhood." I scampered out the door, telling God how thankful I was that I didn't fit into Sally's sensible shoes.

Our conversation was definitely thought-provoking. What would our world look like in a few years? Would our generation continue to stay younger into their sixties and seventies? I had visions of these people and their teenagers playing softball, rollerblading, hiking the Grand Canyon. In other words, keeping up with their kids.

I knew there was no way the baby boomer generation was going to let any young punk outdo them. Not even if they have to use walkers with inline wheels or wear the new, sports style, Depends. Of course, schools will offer CPR as a mandatory course.

Oops...I'm letting my prejudice show. I have to get my thinking clear. I know...I'll take it to God. After all, I've gotten some terrific insights from him.

∾   ∾   ∾   ∾   ∾   ∾

God, what are people thinking? Having children in their middle years? It just seems like it would be so difficult to raise teenagers when you're in your sixties. I don't care how much Centrum Silver you ingest.

A little judgment there?

I guess so. I'm projecting my perspective on others. It's just that the last thing *I'd* want to do is raise a child when I'm

---

in my 50's or 60's. I want my freedom. I want to do what I want to do when I want to do it.

> You *are* a card carrying member of the me generation, aren't you? Yes. You're right. You should be able to do what you want to do. But answer this…shouldn't others be able to do what they want to do when they want to do it?

> I get it!

Up 'til that time, I hadn't considered that other people might actually think differently than me. Whoa…what a concept!

VII. To Wear a Toup Or Not…That Is the Question

Male pattern baldness…

Is it contagious?

So some baby boomers were waiting until mid-life to start their families. An interesting time. I noticed that while these boomer mommies-to-be were getting pregnant, their husbands were losing their hair. What gives? Do you suppose their's a correlation?

After visiting with Sally, I'd talked with a couple other professional women who waited until their middle years to start a family. Having exhausted that topic, I decided it was time to check into the baldness thing and it's impact on a guy's ego. But where to begin? The health club of course. It shouldn't be a problem spotting some interviewees. I'd just follow the light bouncing off their shinny round skulls.

After checking in with my friend Jim, the owner, I wandered around the exercise area. I didn't see Mike-the-charmer-with-the-penile-implant, but I did notice Virginia getting ready to go into the dry sauna. She waved hello, and tugged on the seat of her swimsuit trying to cover rippling mounds of flesh creeping down the leg holes.

Jim had pointed out a guy over in the corner, a little guy, about five-feet-five, but with a terrific body. He also had a full head of hair. I couldn't figure out why Jim had sent me his way, but decided to find out. I sauntered over to him and his barbells, and gave him the usual introduction.

"Hey, that sounds like fun. Are you a writer?"

Duh, no it just sounds like it. "Yes, and I'm focusing on hair loss today. But that doesn't seem to be your problem. Maybe you have some friends who have a hair loss problem."

He kinda ducked his head, and actually blushed. He had a pretty terrific looking head of hair, sandy colored with a few gray streaks here and there. It was an attractive mix. "You really think it looks good?"

It appeared that I was on to something here after all. "Great hair. You haven't by any chance had it...uh...altered in some way? It seems like a popular baby boomer thing to do. You know, that I'll-be-young-and-good-looking-forever-or-die-trying attitude."

He grinned. "I hadn't thought of it that way. But I guess you're right. You see, I had a hair transplant." He started pointing to various parts of his head. My scalp tingled just thinking about it. He pointed to one spot where the hair was particularly curly. "Guess where that batch came from." He was practically gleeful now. I supposed he didn't talk about it to just anyone.

"Gosh, I dunno." He had all this sandy curly hair peeking out from under his T-shirt. "From your chest? Your back?"

He was almost rolling on the floor with laughter. I was starting to get an awful picture. That hair didn't come from his chest or back. It came from where the sun rarely shines. "Okay, I think I'm getting the picture." Men really do have a strange sense of humor. "So how did you come to the decision to do this?"

His momentary collapse into hilarity passing, he regained his composure. Wiping tears of laughter out of his eyes, he started talking more seriously. "Well, I was getting pretty thin up there, and I didn't like it. After all, I'm short to begin with, and I have to make my assets count. You know…most women like tall men. I was working hard at the gym to build the old biceps, but losing the hair was too much."

He ran his hand through his hair. "I went to this doctor, and he convinced me that I could have a hair transplant, just moving a little bit from here to there. That sounded easy enough, so I gave him the go ahead. Man, it hurt like hell. I couldn't put my head on a pillow for a month. Had to sleep sitting up. You ever tried that?

"Then it got worse. He ran out of hair and I still had some blank spots on the noggin. I figured that was it, I was just going to have to tolerate those spots. But this guy was nothing if not creative. Told me to take my clothes off, and looked me over with a fine tooth comb. It was a little embarrassing, I can tell you, what with his nurse standing there watching. This nurse was a big gal, about six feet tall, and had a mustache. Gave me the creeps. Suddenly she lunges forward, pointing to my nether regions. In a low-pitched manly voice, she says, 'There, doctor! There's plenty right there.' The doc looks closer, and says, 'You're right as usual, nurse.'

"The doctor has this big loopy grin on his face, reminding me of some hunter who's hound dog just treed a raccoon. 'She's better than I am, any day of the week. We'll take a patch

There, Doctor! There's plenty right there!

from there, young man, and finish that head off.'"

My guy shook his head. "I didn't think anything could hurt more than that hair transplant, but I was wrong. I couldn't wear anything but jogging pants for two weeks. It was worth it, though. Now I've got a great head of hair, and women love it. Of course, I don't tell them where some of it came from, unless I get the feeling that one of them is extra special. Then I tell 'em. It's kind of a gauge to see what kind of gal they are. If they don't disappear on me, I know they're okay."

I thought I'd heard everything, but this took the cake. Writing this book was opening new vistas of weirdness for me. "That's quite a story. Thanks for sharing it. Good luck with those women." He nodded and returned to his barbells. I scratched my head, thanked God it had hair, and moved on.

I looked around the room for another point of view. My heart skipped a beat. What luck! There was my old friend Paul. Paul and I used to date, years ago during our freshman year in college. I hadn't seen him in forever. He was blonde, tall, athletic looking, and a real hunk back then. I'd heard that he'd married a woman named Sandra and was making a bundle in the P.R. business.

As I approached him from the rear, I noticed he still possessed the same great physique. But something had changed. What was it? Whoops! That beautiful blonde hair had turned into a fringe. He looked like a friar.

"Hey Paul, how's it going?"

"Well, hi there! Haven't seen you in years. What're you up to?"

"Writing a book on baby boomers. You know, all the aging problems we're experiencing."

He nodded his head, and smiled. "I guess there are a few changes as we get older, aren't there?" Suddenly the smile faded and he shrank back a little. "Just what did you want to talk to me about? Has Sandra been talking again at the beauty shop? Just because a man can't stand up and salute the flag occasionally..."

"No," I hastened to reassure him. "Right now I'm talking to men about the 'B' word. You know, baldness."

He relaxed and laughed. "I was just kidding with you,

anyway. No problem in that department, never have had and never will. Doctor says I'll go at it until I'm ninety. I like to kid Sandra about it, though."

Yeah, right I thought. Thank God Sandra got him instead of me. I'm not sure I'd want to go at it with a ninety year old, even if he was my husband. I went on with the interview. "Tell me Paul, how do men feel about baldness? I notice that since I saw you last you've suffered a slight hair loss."

"Slight hair loss! Why, I'm as bald as a cue ball."

"Well, as bald as a cue ball with sideburns and side fuzz. How do you feel about that?"

"I didn't see you after our freshman year. You probably wouldn't have recognized me anyway. The next year my hair went like wildfire. You'd have thought that there were gremlins pulling it out by the roots while I slept, it came out so fast. It wouldn't have been so bad, except the other students kept mistaking me for one of the younger professors. Out of desperation I tried a toupee and thought it looked great.

"Right at that time, I'd met Sandra. On our third date, we went down to the river to swim. After a lot of sweet talk I convinced her to skinny dip. So there we were, buck naked, having a great time. Feeling romantic, I dove under to do a little nibbling, you know, playing 'fish'. Suddenly I heard her screaming and she started kicking wildly at me.

"I quickly surfaced to see what was going on. It seemed that my toup had come off and floated up right under her nose.

Scared her to death. She must have thought a dead body was coming up next to her. Anyway, I had to explain. It was sure embarrassing. We talked it over, and I decided to go 'au naturel' from then on. She said she preferred it. I figured if a fantastic girl like Sandra could live with it, so could I. And I married her."

"That's a great story, Paul. Do you have any friends suffering from male pattern baldness?"

He chuckled. "Well, there's my neighbor, Bud. He's getting fairly thin on top, but still sports some fuzz. A few weeks ago, his daughter got a bright idea from a commercial on television, and bought a can of 'hair' spray. You know - that stuff you spray on your skull to color it, giving the impression of hair.

"While Bud's napping, she gave his shiny spot a couple of puffs from the can. Later, she comes in and exclaims, 'Dad! What happened? Your hair grew in!!' Bud's still half asleep, and stumbles to the mirror. Worse yet, he didn't have his glasses on. He can't believe his eyes. 'It's a miracle! I've got hair!'

"He actually fell down on his knees and started thanking St. Somebody that he'd lit a candle to for the Rogaine he'd been using to work. His wife comes in and takes a good look. Poor Bud. 'Course the kid got grounded for a month, and Bud refuses to take naps on the sofa anymore. Goes into his room and locks the door."

"So, how did you hear this story? I can't imagine that Bud told you."

"You got that right. His wife told my wife, at the beauty shop. She thought it was hilarious. That seems to be where all the good dirt is dished on husbands." He gave a couple of pulls on his rowing machine as if thinking, then stopped. "I guess I'm as bad as the women, but I've got to tell you about Pete. Pete is one of those guys that's balding on top, but refuses to face the music like I did. So, he lets one side grow real long and combs it up and over the top. He lacquers it down with superhold hair spray. Now, everyone knows what the deal is, but Pete just can't let go of his hair 'hat'.

"What makes this even funnier is that Pete works downtown. One day last week I ate lunch with him. We walked back to his office afterward so he could give me some papers. I never considered how Pete's hair might react to those downtown wind currents. Anyway, we headed out the door of the restaurant and toward his office. Then suddenly, Pete races across the street. He's still going in the direction of his office, though. I followed along, trying to keep up. It's like an episode of Cops. (Bad boys, bad boys, what you gonna do when they run from you?) Another block, and Pete runs across the street again. Another block, and he dodges down a side street. I'm getting real curious about these changes.

"This goes on for five blocks, us moving all over between streets. At one point he's practically hugging a building, like Spiderman. I'm beginning to wonder just what kind of a pervert he is. Then, I figured it out."

Frankly, I was mystified. "Okay, I give up. Tell me what

he was up to?"

Now Paul was laughing so hard he could barely talk. "It was that darn hair flap. He has every downtown air current memorized. North on Fifth, light breeze roughly 3-5 knots; South on Fourth, wind reverses direction with gusts up to 7-10 knots; West on Ash, as calm as the Horse Latitudes. He's a sidewalk sailor! He walks where the wind won't catch his hair and hold it straight up, like some hairy horn.

Paul continued, "But once in a while, like that day, the wind currents change and good ol' Pete gets caught. The wind caught his hair flap, and up it went. You should have seen the look on these two teenagers' faces as they went by. They probably thought Pete was copying one of those punk hairdos. I was laughing so hard my sides were about to split. I don't think Pete'll ever forgive me."

I let him calm down a little as I pondered men and their hair foibles. And people say women are vain. This was a big insight for me. But now he was talking about another friend of his. Paul was definitely a bountiful bag of bald tidbits.

"...and in walks John, with hair all of a sudden. Everyone at the meeting had their eyes glued to his noggin, including the CEO. I felt really sorry for the salesman making the presentation. He could have been offering to give the stuff away and we wouldn't have known it. We're all looking in his direction, but transfixed by John. Most of us didn't get one word of his pitch.

"After a while the CEO calls a break and we head for

the restroom, dragging John along with us. I think that if they could have gotten away with it, some of the women would have followed us in also.

"John's enjoying being the center of attention. Then he showed us the most amazing thing. That darn hairpiece was snapped to his head. Click, click, click, and he took it off. Showed us these brass snaps that had been implanted in his scalp. 'No glue for me,' he said. This was the latest thing in toupees. He can play 'fish' all day. We were speechless." Paul was shaking his head, as if still amazed at the memory of that sight. "Can you imagine?"

My mouth was hanging open. No, I couldn't imagine. I had had enough for one day. My scalp literally ached. I said goodbye and left the health club. Out in my car, I started laughing. Tears rolled down my face as I pictured these guys. I was so engrossed in my thoughts that I didn't hear the knocking at my window. I looked up, and saw Virginia (of the Dove Bars).

Rolling down the window, "Hey, Virginia. Going home?" I was trying to stop laughing.

"What's so funny? I don't remember *ever* coming out of there laughing."

"I've been getting men's stories about their hair loss. It's crazy what they'll do to keep the illusion of hair." She sighed. Something in her look captured my attention. I smelled a husband hair story. "Uh, how's your husband's hair doing these days?"

"I'm afraid he's getting balder every day. I miss running my hands through that curly mane he used to have. I'll tell you, it was pretty impressive when we got married. Then, little by little, it started thinning. I didn't say anything when the spot on top got noticeable, knowing how sensitive he was. I mean, he wasn't saying much about my weight gain then, either."

"What happened to change everything?" I asked gently. She was looking very serious, and I could tell this was near to her heart.

Slowly this big grin moved through her chubby features, and I knew we were going to get a good story. "Well, you know how men try to cover up their bald spots by combing the hair from the side over it?"

I nodded, still picturing Pete crisscrossing the streets to avoid his hair horn from getting blown up, like a soldier running a zigzag pattern to keep from getting shot, and then hugging the buildings like a tree frog.

"That's what my husband does. He'll do anything to keep it in place. There's enough mousse on his head to start a lodge. And hair spray? It's as if he's trying to knock his own personal hole in the ozone. But there's one time that it just doesn't hold."

I frowned. "When?" I asked innocently. I hadn't personally experienced this problem and wasn't being very creative.

She was looking mischievous now, like she had a great

big package for me to open. "In bed, of course! He has to keep moving his head just so, or it falls the wrong way. No matter what he does, his first concern is whether his hair is going to stay in place, so he'll look sexy. Let me tell you, sometimes it's all I can do not to burst out laughing right there in the middle of sex, watching him maneuver so that his hair will lay right."

It was hard to contain a new fit of laughter. "I take it, you do a lot of riding on top, then. To make it easier on him, I mean."

She was looking wistful now. "Not really." She glanced down at her mountainous thighs. "I'd probably squish him. Besides, I can't squat low enough to get to his...you know!"

I coughed to suppress a giggle. "So what do you do?"

Virginia looked coy. "Oh, we just work around it." She looked up at the sky. "You know how men like it really tight. Doesn't matter where it's tight."

I wasn't touching that one with a ten foot pole. "Yes, well, I'm finding out that growing older is pretty hard on us baby boomers," I said, as I started my car. "See you later, Viagra...I mean Virginia."

As I drove away, I felt sad. So much vanity. So much ego. So many people into looks. Was this what the baby boomers were all about?

VIII. Prozac - the New Wonder Drug

All psyched up and nowhere to go.

As I thought about all the people I'd been talking to, I realized I hadn't heard much about a prime issue in our group: therapy. We have to be the most meditated, medicated, analyzed, energized, and enervated group of people in history. In the last twenty years, we've been *est*'d, Rebirthed, I'm O.K.'ed - Your Ok'd, sensitized, de-sensitized, primal screamed at, and group therapied, right into Rubber Ramada.

We've been self-helped with everything from hating our parents to kicking our dog. We've swallowed every drug, herb, and Herb that was said to help us. Starting with the hippies, we've been a generation of 'feel-gooders', seeking it through burning our draft cards and our bras, saving the environment, liberating whales, taking drugs, changing religions, and turning into couch potatoes, migrating from one 12-step program to the next.

The more I thought about this, the more I knew I had to talk with God again.

æ   æ   æ   æ   æ   æ

God, I need to talk with you again. And this is really serious.

All our talks are serious. I may kid around...since God is everything, I certainly have a sense of humor...but I always take you seriously.

I appreciate that. I've been very focused on us baby boomers in this book, and I see several themes as I look around. One is that we seem very intent on "finding ourselves". Other generations haven't seemed to be that way. Why us?

> Very good question. Remember, up here time does not exist like it does for you. You have an entirely different perspective because you are so linear. You can't imagine existence any other way. You see life as a progression. An evolution. And, therefore, for you, it is.

What does that have to do with finding ourselves? Are you trying to confuse me again with too much information?

> No...I've never tried to confuse you. That's something you do to each other. I'm trying to tell you that your generation has "evolved" from seeking to meet your most essential physical needs - food, clothing and shelter - to seeking to meet your essential psychological and spiritual needs. The generation after you is

already in that mindset. You see - you piggybacked off each other as your consciousness evolved. It's been quite a program to watch. You've got a big audience rooting for you, you know.

Here we go again! Earth is just one big, ever-lasting commercial-free version of Jerry Springer for the folks on high to enjoy.

No matter what I say, humans twist it around. Why, just look at all the great teaching books I've sent you. The Bible. The Koran. Monica Speaks.

There you go again...making fun of me. I don't think Monica has much to teach...anyway, not anything I want to learn.

I'm just demonstrating a point - humans take life too seriously - lighten up! I may have been responsible for creating humans, but they still constantly amaze me.

So we're a disappointment to you? Is that what you're saying? You sound a lot like some moms I know.

Twist, twist, twist...

æ   æ   æ   æ   æ   æ

After a little thought, I decided that if I was going to explore our psyches, I'd go to the horse's mouth. I called and made an appointment with a psychiatrist that several of my friends had gone to lately. He'd just had a cancellation, and the receptionist invited me to come right on over.

I'd never been to a psychiatrist before, so I expected a leather couch and bearded pipe-smoking pervert, a' la Freud. Apparently, this guy hadn't taken Psychiatrist Office 101 in school. There was no couch, just a normal looking office with comfortable chairs in front of his desk. There was also a little table and two wee chairs. I deduced that he also dabbled with child psychiatry or counseled the occasional munchkin.

The doctor definitely was not an a' la Freud. No beard on this guy. Actually, there wasn't all that much hair anywhere on his finely shaped head. (Too bad I didn't meet him when I was doing research for the chapter on Male Pattern Baldness.) He placed his well-manicured hands on his desk, formed a steeple with his finger tips, and looked me right in the eye. He was middle-aged, possessing the slight paunch of one who sits for a living. "So, what is your problem? How may I help you?"

For about the fiftieth time I began, "I'm writing a book about baby boomers. We seem to be compulsive about the inside of our heads, so I thought I'd ask the expert. Why are so many people of our generation so screwed up? Is it the chlorine in the water? The fluoride in our toothpaste? The Clinton's in the White House? What's your professional opinion?"

The doctor looked non-plussed. "You mean you're not a patient? Did my receptionist know this? Do you know what my rates are?"

I gulped. "How about if I give you credit in the foreword? The receptionist said that you had a cancellation anyway."

He relaxed a little. "Well, if I get credit in the book. But make sure you quote me correctly. I don't want to sound like an idiot. After all, you're only a layman, and don't know the jargon. That kind of thing can ruin a career."

I got my notebook out and tried to look competent. "So, what's up with this boomer generation?"

He assumed a professional air and began to expound pompously. "If you want my bottom line (good, I thought, that's the area most boomers seem to be focused on) opinion, these people have too much. Back when the general population's life was rural in nature and lives were relatively simple, there were fewer options, and cultural expectations were quite inhibiting. Now, people are surrounded by electronics, gadgets, and expensive name brands. The poorest of the poor have these expectations. It makes for an unhappy home."

I nodded appreciatively. "So, you feel that if we could return to a simpler, easier time, our little psyches would also calm down and revert to their former dull, albeit satisfied, selves."

His face lit up excitedly. "You get it! I'm surprised. Most regular folks," and here he had the grace to blush condescendingly, "don't understand. You're obviously not one of the great unwashed mob out there." He leaned forward in his maroon leather chair. "Have you ever been in therapy? I could,"

You're obviously not one of the great unwashed mob.

he coughed quietly, "give you some gratuitous sessions. I find you uh...rather interesting."

The look on his face was not showing professional interest right now. Like I said earlier in the book, I may be fifty, but I still get a come-on once in a while. Mike, with-the-penile-implant, all over again.

I stood up. "Thank you, but I feel pretty mentally healthy right now. Maybe another time." He shrugged, and looked sort of pouty. I checked to make sure I had his name spelled correctly, then exited. Funny how clean and clear the air seemed back on the street.

I didn't feel satisfied with my conversation with Dr. Big Headd. He hadn't really given me the information I sought. As I walked down the street, I noticed a sign on a building announcing "Feelings R' Us Therapy Group". Below the name it said, "Play Therapy For Your Inner Child."

I ignored the rumblings in my stomach that said it was lunchtime and entered. Any group with this kind of motto had to be helpful.

Inside a receptionist sat at a bright red desk. There were lots of primary colored pillows around, and some huge plastic crayons leaning against the wall, like a Romper Room flashback. I half expected Miss Sally to come out. As I started to ask some questions, a woman came out with her handbag. (She didn't look at all like Miss Sally. So much for childhood illusions.) "I'm going to lunch, Barbara. Be back in an hour." The receptionist flagged her down. "This lady needs some help. Could you talk to her?"

Her name was Adrianna, and once she heard my mission, she asked if I wanted to go to lunch with her. My stomach thanked her, and we ended up down the street in a small deli, Kraut an' Lick.

We ordered, and Adrianna mused on some of her weirder cases. "Let me tell you about some cases I've had you might appreciate. These are people from my practice in WallaWalla, so I'm not breaking confidentiality. You'll disguise them, won't you?"

"Of course." Underneath the table I crossed my fingers. This book was getting longer all the time and disguising people takes a lot of work.

"There was Robert (name changed from Bob to protect his identity). He had some very unusual neurotic habits. For instance, he would lick women's hands. Mostly on dates, of course. When he started doing it in the business world, he came for help. His boss was going to fire him otherwise."

I didn't particularly like the vision. "That's disgusting," was my comment.

Adrianna smiled and bit into her Reuben sandwich. She chewed, then continued. "It gets worse. He had a leather fetish. Would even chew on his date's shoes and sniff around their toilets." She giggled a little at my completely appalled countenance. "I know. Pretty bad. When he came to me, he'd been to some psychiatrist who 'dug up' this repressed memory of his mother giving all of her attention to her three dogs instead of to him. He had to compete, so took up doggy behaviors. (I wondered if he'd ever been injured chasing cars.) After that, he very conveniently blamed Mom for *all* his troubles."

"Gee," I said. "What a terrible childhood for the poor guy."

"You haven't heard the kicker. After working with him for a while, I decided to do some research and checked around about his childhood. Get this - his mom never had any dogs. He was an only child and he had loads of attention. Every one I talked to concurred. They can't figure out where he got this stuff."

I was writing like crazy. "Go on," I urged.

"Then there was the invisible man. He'd broken his nose twelve times from trying to walk through walls."

"Just a minute," I said. "The invisible man couldn't walk through walls. He was just invisible."

"Tell that to this guy. They make up their own neuroses, you know. His nose was as big and red as an apple from all those breaks. Reminded me of W.C. Fields." She shook her head.

"I was having one of those years, because after him, I

came across the compulsive flusher. He'd drop things into the john so that he could flush and watch as they swirled round and round. Stood there for hours flushing. Between missing work to prolong his flushing fancy and using tons of water, it got to the point that he couldn't afford to pay his water bill. After several warnings, the water company fixed his flushing fancy by cutting off his water, creating the great flushing fancy finale."

"Did he get better after his toilet flushing frenzy faded?" I wondered.

"No. Worse. He turned to salad oil."

"What did he do with it? Pour it in the toilet?"

"Nope. Poured it on the hall floor. (I prayed the floor wasn't carpeted.)

Even my fertile brain was stumped by that one. "What on earth did he do that for?!"

"He wanted to return to his childhood memories. The Slip and Slide came to mind immediately. But he was afraid the neighbors would see him, so he opted for an indoor version. Fun, huh?"

I was seeing a very sick side of the baby boomers. "Why do you think they do these things? Are there more sick people than there used to be? A psychiatrist I talked to says that it's because we have too much 'stuff'."

Adrianna pondered this for a moment. We'd finished

our sandwiches and were considering the chocolate chip cookies at the checkout counter. Speaking of too much stuff.

"The official line at our office is that we're buying toys to satiate that broken inner child who will never be satisfied. But personally, I think the inner child is becoming a bit spoiled."

We parted. I ambled down the street contemplating Adrianna's remarks. Were we spoiled? Had we sold our souls to chase the American Dream? You know - the one we thumbed our noses at in the 60's and early 70's. I wondered.

IX. God...Help Me!!

Why am I here?

Yes, it seemed most of the baby boomers I'd
interviewed were concerned with finding the

fountain of youth. They were concerned with their looks, their money, their cars, everything outside of themselves. I was feeling a driving need to look beneath this facade, and hoped I'd find that we are more than a bunch of aging, shallow, former hippies who sold out to the man for a house in the burbs, a golden retriever in the yard, and a younger partner in the sack. I went to see Jennifer. After all, she was my first appointment.

She wasn't on the StairMaster this time. She was lying on the sofa, feet up, an icepack on her head. Her eyes were puffy and red. She looked like hell. (I felt good.)

"Jennifer, what gives? You look like you just lost your best friend."

She gave me a Look. I knew that Look. Her guy was gone. "He left me. For a twenty-five year old waitress at the health club on the edge of town." I remembered the blonde that Julio, Virginia's personal trainer, had been talking to when I was last there. "Is she blonde?" I asked. "Yeah, I think so," was the reply.

She continued, a much more serious and insecure Jennifer than I had talked to before. "I thought I had it all. Beauty, intelligence, and money in the bank. Terrific body, and terrific man. It was like I had a picture in the closet. You know, like Dorian Gray. But in the end, all those things go, don't they?"

I sighed. It was too sad. I related something that my

minister, Brenda, once said. "You can't hitch a U-Haul to the hearse. All of our material possessions and all of our attempts at trying to stay young don't mean much when we're on the way to our grave. For instance, your butt tuck..."

She looked horrified. "Who told you about my butt? I didn't think anyone knew!"

I looked innocent. What's a writer to do? Reveal my sources? No way! But, now Jennifer was running to the phone. Dialing. Fuming. "Melissa!" she raged. "Did you tell about my butt tuck? You're the only one who knew." Silence for a moment. She was listening. Her face grew pale. I was afraid she was going to have a stroke. She dropped the phone without even hanging up, and ran to her computer. Two minutes later she was surfing the Net, looking intently for something. She evidently found it. (A pause.) She slumped to the floor in a dead faint. I was shocked. I didn't think women swooned anymore. Fortunately a little water on the face brought her around.

"I'm dead. I can never go anywhere again. How humiliating." I looked over at the computer. There was a picture of two bare butts on the screen.

"Is that...uhh...you?"

"It sure is. Can you believe the nerve of that doctor? Doing a case history of my butt and putting it on the Internet? Everyone in kingdom come will know. I'll never have another date in my life."

"I don't know," I surmised, admiring the doctor's handiwork. "This might get you a lot of dates. And - besides, you must have signed a release to have your butt spread (pun) all over the web."

Whining, "I signed so many papers, I quit reading after the first paragraph." She groaned and returned to her prone position. "Besides, what does it matter now - my life is over."

I hesitated. "Jennifer, remember what we were just starting to talk about? You go to the New Age church down the street, don't you? What does it teach?"

Jennifer's anguish seemed to diminish a little as she pondered this question. "You're right. I've been so self-absorbed. I guess I was afraid that if I really admitted I was getting older, and not young and perfect anymore, no one would want me. It's been me, me, me. That's not what our belief system is at all." She looked rueful. "What a lesson. Why do they have to hurt so much?"

(Watch this God, ol' boy.)

(Go get 'em girl!)

I smiled. "Maybe because when they come as little messages, we ignore them. Apparently, we have to get clobbered over the head so that we get the picture. Anyway, that's the way it seems to me."

"You're right." She bounced back up. "I feel much better." She looked in the mirror. "I don't look *that* bad, do I?"

"No, Jennifer. You look just great." And…wondering if in the end (no pun intended) she had really gotten the message. One step forward, two steps back. I left.

I hadn't found what I wanted. I felt like Jennifer was trying, but was still wanting her body to carry her. Where were the baby boomers on a deeper path? Were there any (besides me)?

I walked back towards the coffee house. The smell of fresh baked bread lured me into a bagel shop instead. Sarah came bouncing in. Literally. Waving her over, I watched in amazement when she sat down and literally dusted the table off with her chest. I wondered whether she ever sprayed her bra with Endust. It would save a lot of time around the house. "Hey, how's it going?"

"Fine," I answered. "I was just thinking about God. I have conversations with him sometimes. You wouldn't believe what he says. I guess you think that's weird, though."

Sarah giggled. "How do you know God's a he? I prefer to think he's a she. Or maybe even an it. Who knows?"

I remembered the conversation I'd had with him where he declared he's really an essence.

Sarah continued her thoughts. "I even talked to God before I had my boob job. She gave me the go ahead. Meta-physically, of course."

"I've lost you. How did God tell you metaphysically to

have your boobs done?" I couldn't wait to hear this one!!

"I knew she'd give me a sign, one way or another. I'll never forget it. I'd gone hiking on my favorite trail, and got to the place where there's a stream by a little meadow. I laid down and closed my eyes, just daydreaming. Suddenly I heard the coo of a dove, and opened my eyes. Up in the sky were all these clouds, moving really fast. I was fascinated, watching them curve, one into another. Have you ever done that?"

I was really into this story and wanted the punchline. "Yeah, I know what you mean. But get on with it. What was the sign?"

"Well, the clouds kept moving, and then I saw it. The sign. Two big clouds shaped like breasts in the sky, just hanging up there for all the world to see. They looked like Dolly Parton's, or Marilyn Monroe's. I knew then that mine were meant to be. (Thank goodness she hadn't seen clouds in the shape of male genitals.)

"I jumped up, ran down the trail, and drove into town, straight to the plastic surgeon's office. Even though it was Saturday, I just knew he'd be there. After all, I was acting from Divine guidance. As I suspected, he was there - working on some woman. I marched right in, threw open the door and announced, 'I want those, just like her's!' Turned out it was his wife! Boy, you should talk to her. She's out to here."

She modeled with her hands. I got the picture. "So that

was your message from God."

"Always talk to God. You have to trust. It's the only way to live life." (Yeah. That and watch the Weather Channel.)

I agreed. It was good to hear it from another baby boomer, though. Reaffirming. Maybe there's hope for us after all. Of course, she didn't know that I'd already talked to Patrick's wife, Vicky. It certainly was a small world. Sarah bid farewell and bounced away.

I stayed at the table, musing about Sarah's sign from God. I wondered how many other baby boomers had had such an experience. Ah! Serendipity. In strolled John, a stalwart Baptist who attended church every Sunday. He spotted me and headed for my table.

I vividly remember attending his baptism. They held him under for what seemed like an unusually long time. Just as I became concerned, he exploded out of the water, wearing a smile so big, you'd swear maybe he was the one who'd had a face lift. I couldn't wait to corner him and find out what the big grin was about. He told me he'd had a vision of an angel telling him he would be paving the way for a special person who would speak to throngs of people.

I didn't have the heart to tell him that sounded like he'd confused himself with "John the Baptist." (Maybe they did hold him under a little too long.) Today there was no smile.

"John, you look troubled."

I've had a vision! I've seen the light!

"I am. I'm wondering what my life's really about."

"You surprise me. I thought you'd figured it out."

"I thought so too. Not so. The questions are coming up stronger than ever. Questions like, 'Why am I here?' 'What's my life all about?' 'Is chocolate ice cream really bad for me?'" His plaintive voice begged for answers.

"This is very interesting John. I'm writing a book on how baby boomers are aging and how most of them seem to be concerned with what's outside of themselves, rather than what's inside. Then along you come asking the big 'why' questions.

I'm heartened to learn you're asking, but surprised you haven't already found the answers. What gives?"

John seemed a bit uncomfortable, fidgeting in his chair. Finally, he leaned over and in a hushed tone, "You remember when I was baptized?"

"Yes. I thought they were going to drown you."

"Remember my vision?"

"Yes."

"Well, I've spent the last ten years looking for that person who would come forth to speak to the throngs. As a result, I've been paying mighty close attention to the Bible stories I've been hearing at church. Since I have an inquisitive mind, I've noticed that their stories don't make sense.

"For instance, if God gave us free will, why is there hell to pay when we exercise it? If Jesus really said that we'd do even greater things than he did, why does the church try to make everyone feel inferior to him? And, if God really spent all that much time talking to people back then, why haven't we heard from him in the last thousand or so years? (I tried to hide a smirk at that one.) These are only a few of the many questions. There's loads of inconsistencies."

"Sounds like you've been using your logic. (Bad choice.) You have some valid points there. And, knowing you, I'm sure you won't rest until you have the answers."

"That's why I came over when I spotted you. You seem

to have a fairly comfortable approach to life and I thought you might give me some clues. Actually, I've been thinking about calling you for a month now, but never got around to it. And here you are. Go figure."

"You know - I was thinking the same thing when you showed up. How can I help?"

John looked frustrated. "I thought you might share some of your insights."

"Trust me. You want to find your own answers." Besides, I thought, he could buy the book like everyone else.

I empathized with John. I knew how difficult it was for me when I began to question the religion I'd grown up in. When the light came on, I realized I'd been manipulated by fear, and it simply didn't feel right. Nevertheless, I felt that John would be better off finding his own answers.

"I'm sure you're right. I've spent the last ten years believing someone else's version of God. I can't believe it took me so long to ask some very basic and logical questions."

"Better late than never." Gees, I hate cliches. "I'll give you one clue about God and about life - I believe we're here to experience joy. After all, God made this world so there must be a reason, and there must be a reason we're occupying it. If I were you, I'd start my investigation into the possibility of a synergistic relationship between God and humans. One more thing - don't believe that Adam and Eve story. I have it on good authority that it wasn't to be taken literally."

"Thanks."

I motioned the waitress over to pay the tab. Finally, I felt financially fit and picked up John's tab also.

John and I drifted out of the bagel shop and walked together to the corner. He turned right and I turned left. I knew I'd done the right thing. He must find his own way.

X. You Mean It's Okay to Enjoy Life?

Even though I felt like I'd done the right thing by not answering John's questions, his mood triggered a feeling of melancholy within me. I don't much care for that feeling, knowing we're on this earth to experience joy. But sometimes you have to indulge those sad feelings, at least for a couple of minutes. Well, time for another check in with "you know who."

આ   આ   આ   આ   આ   આ

You know, my friend John is pretty disheartened right now.

John who?

Very funny. I won't go into detail because I'm sure you know his story. It's not uncommon. And then there's all these other people I've been talking with. Most of them don't even have a clue. It seems they're focusing on the appearance of their bodies, on their cars, on money, but have neglected their spirituality. Are the baby boomers really that shallow?

No, you're not shallow. It's just that when you incarnate into the human form, you believe you're separate from me. You keep looking at your bodies and seeing them as solid. You're having a difficult time realizing that you're first, and foremost, a spiritual being, and that we are one. You don't understand that I'm the energy that flows through you. But each of you will eventually have your own experience of reconnection, of knowing our oneness. Of course it might happen after death..."

You know, that's one of your lesser inventions...

Oh, you think so huh? Well, if you didn't go through that death thing, you'd still be walking on all fours. Actually, some of you act as if you should be walking on all fours.

You're so funny. (I'm wondering who this is? The God I was raised with didn't talk like this. I haven't heard one "thou shalt" or even more to the point, one "thou shalt not" since I started talking with him.)

That's right, I am funny. Who do you think was the original comedian? Thank you very much. I'll be here for eternity. Try the veal. Anyway, because each person must come to their own experience, won't you agree that John's pretty fortunate about now? He's asking the questions that lead to within. In fact, all those who begin asking are given the answers.

They may come in any number of ways, through teachers, books (you'll be happy to know), friends, clouds, etc. You simply must be open to the information. Some of you expect a burning bush or "tablets a' la Moses". It ain't gonna happen. Not in this generation, anyway.

Why not?

Any idea what the paperwork looks like for an environmental study to burn a bush or two?

There you go again...always the comedian. Yes. I know you're right. Of course, you're always right. Or *are* you? What about dinosaurs? Did you decide they were just a bad idea and erase them suddenly? (Of course listening to Barney, I can see why you would have gotten rid of them.) Or how about the Neanderthal man? I haven't noticed many of those running around lately, except in Washington D.C. Did you decide they were too hairy?

When they were passing out wisecracks you got more than your fair share, didn't you? I guess that's what makes a good writer, though. For your information, dinosaurs were perfect. And if you don't believe me, I've got two words for you - fossil fuels. After all, you wouldn't have any gas and oil to run your cars if it weren't for their poor decaying bodies. And how could they have made those great movies if it weren't for the dinosaurs? Remember Godzilla? Same for the Neanderthal. That idea has produced some really good literature, not to mention giving a lot of archeologists work.

I just wish people would realize sooner that we're an extension of you and we're here for joy.

Why not write a book? (Tee hee.)

Wise ass. Oops. Sorry. I forgot who I was talking to. You just sounded like one of the boys.

What do you think I've been saying? Don't you find joy when you're totally absorbed in something you love? Like archeology, or making fun movies like *King Kong*? It doesn't matter what work you do as long as you're enjoying it. It doesn't even

You mean my highest purpose is fossil fuel?

matter if you realize our oneness, as long as you're enjoying your life. Everything you do is perfect. Even looking outside yourselves for the answers is perfect. In the end you always find the truth. Even if it's at death, like I said earlier.

There are no mistakes. You can see that when you look back at the dinosaurs, since you used them as an example. The big picture is so huge you can't begin to grasp it. If you'd lived during the time of the dinosaurs or Neanderthal, you wouldn't have seen the benefit. But now that you're eons from that point in time, you should be able to see why their extinction was part of the plan. Eons from now, you would be able to see the necessity of current events and realize that they really weren't as devastating as you now believe them to be.

Okay. Alright. I'm starting to catch a glimpse of the big picture. I'm sitting here worrying about my screw-ups. You're saying I should be focusing on joy rather than judging myself and my peers. But it's a little difficult not to judge myself when everyone else does.

You're right. You could write a book about yourselves and call it *Here Come the Judge. Stop it!!* That's an order from God. (Hah! Hah!) No, just kidding. You have free will. You're so free, you can even judge yourselves silly if it gives you a good time. God won't rain on your parade, because I know you'll eventually realize your perfection and love yourselves as I do.

I get it. We're free to do anything, even truly love ourselves. And when we choose to love ourselves, other things start working in our lives. When we begin looking at the perfection of our lives rather than judging everything around us, we get more perfection in our lives. I'm beginning to understand, love is a boomerang. When we send out love, we get it back.

You're becoming very insightful. *Finally!* But you said your publisher's waiting for this book. Shouldn't we wrap this up?

Well, when we started this conversation, about an hour ago, I was asking about joy. Yeah, I know there's no time where you are, but yes, I do have a schedule. The publisher *is* waiting on this book. But I have to know, when does the joy part come in?

When you're living your life knowing our oneness, you live from joy. You see the beauty in the earth, in each other. You understand the miracle that each of you are. When you live in joy, your life seems to go the way you wish it to. Or when you hit a Trifecta at Del Mar. Kidding.

As usual, you've given me more than I knew I wanted! But I like the challenge and look forward to many more conversations with you.

❧   ❧   ❧   ❧   ❧   ❧

That's it! I got it! What God said was true. Baby boomers came here in mass, to evoke change. Yeah. We have made a dramatic change in people's consciousness. We chose to look at life differently. We even stopped a war. Then we got involved with living life. Chasing after careers. Having babies. Raising families. Exercising. But even in these pursuits, we've had a dramatic impact on society's thoughts about aging. We've determined that we're not going to accept the established stigmas of growing older.

At the same time, it's evident that we've neglected our spirituality. Now, people like John are again asking the difficult questions - "Why am I here?" "What's this all about?"

If I understand the concepts I just heard, life's about focusing on *joy* and *love*.

Maybe that's where the real fountain of youth resides, in finding joy in everyday life. Or, maybe I need to talk to more of my friends (if I have any left) about the love and joy aspect. I guess God's right, another book!

You mean the fountain of youth lies within?!

Aleta Pippin
The Institute for
Authentic Entrepreneuring

Unleash the wild entrepreneur within you. Take control of your future. Become an Authentic Entrepreneur.

An Authentic Entrepreneur is one who assesses their core values and creates a meaningful business and lifestyle based on aligning those values with their feelings and their dreams.

Visit <http://www.authenticentrepreneur.com> for information about workshops and products.

Order Form

To order copies of ***Yikes!! My Butt's Falling***, fill out and mail this form along with your check or credit card information to:

Inner Sources Publishing
P. O. Box 8569
La Jolla, CA 92038

or call **800-686-0923**

_____copies of Yikes!! My Butt's Falling @ $14.95 =_____

(CA residents add 7.75% sales tax)   Tax (if any) = _____

($4 for first book, $.50 for each
additional book)   Shipping & Handling = _____

TOTAL = _____

Name: _____
Company: _____
Address:_____
City: _____
State:_____Zip:_____
Telephone:_____
            Credit Card Information: ❏ Visa   ❏ MasterCard

Card Number:_____
Name on Card:_____
Expiration Date:_____
Signature:_____

For wholesale discounts, call 800-686-0923
For more information visit our web site <http://www.innersources.com>